antonio carluccio
goes wild

antonio carluccio
goes wild

with photographs by William Shaw

HEADLINE

I dedicate this book, with pleasure, to my step-grandson Theo Patrick, aged three. In fact he calls me Grandpa Cep, to distinguish me from the other two. The very sweet boy was born on the way to the hospital in a Renault Espace, probably because he was in such a hurry to arrive in this world. Judging by how seriously he takes eating good food – and even though I was not genetically involved in his making – I believe that he will make a great gourmet...at least I hope so.

ACKNOWLEDGEMENTS
My thanks to the following people and organisations for all their help in the production of this book:

Susan Fleming
Kate Habershon
Alastair Hendy
Heather Holden-Brown
Lorraine Jerram
Isobel Gillan
William Shaw
Timothy Neat
Wild Harvest
Graham at Portwine
Diana Bateman
Giselle Blake-Davies
Priscilla Carluccio, for tasting and advising
Enza Bettelli
Alvaro Maccioni
Tim Winter
Drew McPherson
David Thomas
Claudio Bincoletto
Italiana Capers Sud

Photographs © 2001 William Shaw except for pp.154, 164 © Heather Angel; pp.196, 204, 211, 214, 218 © Bruce Coleman Collection; pp.68, 72 © Timothy Neat; p.152 © Philip Steele/ICCE; pp.113, 116, 119 © David E. Thomas; and pp.121,122,123 © Tim Winter

First published in 2001
by HEADLINE BOOK PUBLISHING

10 9 8 7 6 5 4 3 2 1

British Library Cataloguing in Publication Data
   Carluccio, Antonio
   Antonio Carluccio goes wild:120 fresh recipes
     for wild food from land and sea
   1. Cookery
   I. Title
   641.5

ISBN 0 7472 7589 0

Edited by Susan Fleming
Design and art direction by Isobel Gillan
Photography by William Shaw
Home economy by Kate Habershon
Food styling and photographic art direction
   by Alastair Hendy

Printed and bound in Great Britain by
Butler & Tanner Ltd,
Frome, Somerset

HEADLINE BOOK PUBLISHING
A division of Hodder Headline
338 Euston Road
London NW1 3BH

www.headline.co.uk
www.hodderheadline.com

contents

introduction

The 'wild food' of today cannot be compared with that of yesterday. For our forefathers, hunting and gathering from the wild was a necessity, often their only source of food. For us nowadays it can represent a pleasant hobby or, in the case of some country dwellers who collect certain specialist wild items for sale, an extra source of income. For me personally, going into the country, to places where nature has not yet been domesticated, still represents an enormous pleasure. It's the lure of the chase, where my skills are pitted against those of a nature that will secrete a succulent mushroom under a camouflage of leaves, or a clump of wild garlic in the dark dampness of a wood in spring.

My childhood was spent in Piedmont, in the north of Italy where, amongst the vineyards and farmers' fields, there were still tracts of uncultivated land or woods, where the ground cover and trees were still completely natural and one could collect all sorts of wild foods. My siblings and I were taught by the grown-ups to recognise and gather foods such as wild rocket, dandelion and other herbs and greens, mushrooms, nuts and all sorts of wild fruits and berries. When on holiday at the seaside, I was introduced to the bounty available in the sea itself and along the shoreline, the variety of fish and shellfish that, from unpolluted waters, were there for the taking. (Collecting, though, can occasionally be uncomfortable, as I once discovered to my cost. Not having a basket in which to transport some wonderful black mussels, I put them inside my bathing trunks. I was unaware that, as they were still alive, they would attach themselves to anything in the vicinity… A painful experience, but a good nature lesson as well!) And over the intervening years – over twenty-five of them in England – I have continued my exploration of nature, discovering many new varieties of wild food (some of which I discuss here), and strengthening my knowledge of others. For instance I always know where I can find fungi – it may surprise you to learn that I know of a place in London's Hyde Park where every year I can collect giant puffball mushrooms!

The most important element in the search for wild foods, though, is knowledge. You must be able to properly and safely identify plant foods, especially when dealing with fungi. You can learn from books, of course, but direct experience of collecting is an education in itself, preferably at the side of an expert who can guide you along the way. Cooking your wild finds too requires some experience – as well as passion and imagination!

However, I find it a great sadness that the clear distinction between 'wild' and 'cultivated' foods has begun to be eroded (and not just in the game area, see page 183). Supermarkets, that exist to distribute all sorts of foods from all over the world to millions of people, are beginning to offer a few items of wild food such as fungi. Although I like the aspirational idea that almost anyone can get hold of almost anything, I don't think supermarkets should sell foods that are found only occasionally and that are not cultivated. Supermarkets require product lines in quantity, and this could mean stripping wild sources of supply and/or initiating cultivation, which defeats the whole object. I would also be nervous about the staff, who may not have the necessary expertise to give recommendations for correct usage.

And this venturing of large food concerns into the 'wild' area raises other potential horrors. Foods for supermarkets are often produced intensively, providing a good appearance and longer shelf life, but not necessarily the best flavour. Science can step in here, by trying to intervene and develop these attributes in foods humanly produced. Genetic modifications of any kind go against every instinct I possess concerning food and nutrition. And quantity rather than quality is anathema to me. I shall always prefer produce from the wild – an occasional seasonal treat – or the produce offered in almost every French or Italian market.

But all is not lost. Thankfully, in the last few years there have been movements back towards the old and valid ways of rearing animals and growing food plants. The organic movement is fast gaining momentum, and there has been an adverse reaction to many food production methods currently employed. People are re-evaluating, thinking back to healthier and happier times and, most importantly, the present generation is learning to appreciate the more natural ways in which we used to live, cultivate and eat.

By wild food, I mean all edible plants, shoots, leaves, berries, nuts, fungi and fruits growing freely which are not cultivated by human beings. Although I also include game and fish, which are foods with their origins in the wild, under no circumstances do I recommend hunting, shooting or fishing without permission or licences. This also applies to trespassing on private land. This book is intended to be a guide to finding and using selected wild foods as we do in Italy, but for pleasurable enjoyment only, not for survival.

During the last two-thirds of my life, I have lived in large cities, but I have never lost my contact with nature and her wild foods. My mushroom-picking forays are quite well known, I believe, and our house in the country in Hampshire is a sanctuary at weekends, my umbilical cord to the nature I still love so much. Over the years I have learned to respect, love and appreciate nature in all her aspects. I hope you can learn to do the same.

introduzione

Thumbstick Making

It is interesting in life how something apparently insignificant can grow into a major, absorbing hobby, which doesn't require any expenditure but simply a love of nature, good observation skills and patience. It all started when I was very young and toddled along behind an expert collector of mushrooms and wild food. This man, a friend of my father's, taught me how to choose straight wooden sticks with a fork at the top. The fork is important not only as a thumb rest, but to defend yourself against serpentine encounters and to turn over a leaf that might just hide a new mushroom.

The first stick I owned had my initials carved on it with a penknife. I later learned to cut off part of the bark on thumbsticks, to create simple and sometimes quite complex patterns. I now have a collection of more than 300 sticks, each one different, and using different woods from all over the world. Some forty of these hang on the wall of my restaurant in Neal Street, Covent Garden, and customers are always most intrigued as to their origins – Aboriginal or African?

To begin your new hobby, you will need a small foldable wood saw, secateurs and a medium Swiss Army knife with a sharp blade. The best time to collect wood for your sticks is in the autumn or winter, when there is no foliage. Hazelnut trees have long, straight and quick-growing branches with few side shoots. Find a straight stick with a fork at the top, and of a height that will suit you (you can of course cut it down if too long). As a rule, when you are holding the stick, the forearm should be at a 90 degree angle, resting horizontally. The thickness of the base shouldn't be more than 2.5cm (1 in) in diameter. Once you have cut the stick to the right height, cut the top branches of the fork to 10cm (4 in) long, which will make a V shape large enough to hold your thumb comfortably.

Study the characteristics of the stick for a few days before you begin to carve. It is most important that the blade is very sharp and that your hand is very steady. Remember that to obtain a pattern that goes perfectly round a stick, you must count the spaces and divide by 2 or other even numbers (4, 6, 8, 10). If this is not done, you won't make a perfect join at the other side of the stick, nor will the pattern work. This is especially important if you wish to create a chequered pattern, which is made by pressing the knife into the bark in perfect circles at the desired distance apart, and then dividing these sections into squares, cutting vertically. You then lift the bark squares alternately with the knife to obtain the desired effect.

Once the stick has been carved, let it rest for a few days to dry out. If it bends a little during this time, you can remedy this by heating the section under very hot running water and then bending it in the opposite direction on a strong surface (protected by a towel). After a few months you can then smooth the surface of the stick with extremely fine sandpaper, and apply a small amount of furniture wax.

Another 'tool' that has proved to be of vital importance when collecting wild food is a stick with a hook. This enables you to hook down the branches of elderberry and blackberry bushes, or hazelnut trees, so that it is possible to collect the fruits higher up the tree without damaging anything. To cut such a hook, choose a stick which is part of a fork, one side short, the other a long handle of about 1.5m (5 ft) long. Cut away all the little side branches to leave a smooth and possibly straight handle with the hook at the end.

verdure

GREENS

CHLOROPHYLL, WHICH FORMS THE MAJOR PART OF THE GREEN PIGMENTATION of plants, is the life-support system of almost all of nature (with the exception of fungi). The sun's rays are absorbed by the chlorophyll in plants – through the process of photosynthesis – and are transformed into carbohydrate energy to enable the plants to grow and survive.

Nowadays, no-one stops to think about where a simple salad leaf has originated. It arrives cleaned and enveloped in transparent plastic, ready to eat. But many of the beneficial elements will have been stripped from the plants through that packaging, through storage, and through time itself. Greens that you have grown yourself are preferable – and greens that you have plucked from the wild are by far the most satisfying in terms of flavour and economy. In this chapter I show you how it is possible to cook with these wild greens, ending up with delicious dishes that have cost virtually nothing to produce. And I also very much like the idea of using greens that are generally looked down upon as weeds – cooking them is one way of getting back at them! But in order to collect greens from the wild, you will need a basic knowledge of plants, their seasons and their edibility. Not all greens are edible, and some can actually be harmful, so you must be careful.

BORRAGINE

BORAGE *Borago officinalis*

An erect annual herb native to southern Europe, borage is now naturalised all over warm to temperate zones around the world. It was spread throughout Europe by the Romans – as were so many herbs – and is cultivated in the south of England, although it can often be seen growing wild as a herb garden escape in waste land near houses. The plant can grow to about 30–60cm (1–2 ft) in height. All of it is hairy – stems, leaves etc. – and these hairs can actually hurt you when touched. The stems are hollow, and the large, green furry leaves are oval and pointed in shape. Wonderful pendant, blue star-shaped flowers appear from June to September, before the plant forms seeds (it is self-seeding). Bees love borage flowers – so much so that an alternative English name for the plant is 'bee-bread' – and occasionally in England you can find a pure borage honey.

Borage has been associated with 'courage' since Roman times – the name is thought to come from the Latin *borra* or 'rough hair' – and the plant has always been recommended in herbals to ease depression. In fact French homeopathic doctors include a borage-derived drug in the treatment of many nervous disorders. The leaves taste of cucumber, and this does have a palpable 'cooling' effect in the mouth.

In parts of Europe, the stems of borage are cooked and eaten as a vegetable, but in general it is the leaves and flowers that are used. Young leaves – which are less hairy – are good in salads, or they or older leaves can be boiled like spinach (when the hairs disappear); I like to then fry the boiled leaves in olive oil and finish them off with a little lemon juice. *Borragine* leaves are used in Liguria together with other wild herbs and leaves to make a filling for a tummy-shaped ravioli, *pansôti al preboggion*. They have a borage soup in Naples, and the leaves can flavour a vinegar. The flowers are used as well, in Italy as fritters, which are delicious hot or cold with drinks. In Britain the flowers have long been an ingredient of a classic claret-cup, but are now more commonly used in that fruit salad of a summer drink, Pimms. They can also be candied.

BISTECCA DI BORRAGINE

BORAGE SANDWICH

Borage leaves are very substantial, ideal for making this dish, which was suggested by my sister Anna in Italy. It can be either a starter or main course, depending on the size of the leaves.

SERVES 4

8 tender, fresh borage leaves, washed
2 medium eggs
2 tbsp coarsely chopped fresh dill
plain flour

55g (2 oz) Parmesan cheese, freshly grated
olive oil for shallow-frying
1 lemon, quartered
salt and pepper to taste

Shake most of the water from the borage leaves, which should be the size of an open hand. Beat the eggs, and add salt and pepper along with the dill.

Dip 2 leaves at a time into the flour, shaking off any excess. Then dip them into the egg on both sides. Sprinkle one side of one of the leaves with a quarter of the cheese, and then join it to the other by pressing gently to form a 'sandwich'. Shallow-fry in the oil until golden on both sides. Repeat to make 3 more sandwiches.

Serve hot with a lemon quarter and perhaps a few extra fresh borage leaves scattered on top.

MINESTRA DI BORRAGINE

BORAGE STEW

This is a speciality of the Neapolitan area, where they use borage to make a delicious *minestra*, to be accompanied by *crostini* or good bread, toasted.

SERVES 4

600g (1 lb 5 oz) borage leaves
200g (7 oz) Neapolitan hot sausage, thickly sliced
6 tbsp olive oil
1 garlic clove, sliced
1 small chilli, finely chopped (optional)

10 cherry tomatoes, chopped
400ml (14 fl oz) chicken or beef stock
85g (3 oz) Pecorino cheese, freshly grated
salt to taste

Clean the borage leaves, then coarsely chop them. Slice the sausage thickly, then fry in the olive oil for a few minutes on each side. Add the garlic and chilli (if using) and fry for 30 seconds. Add the tomatoes, stock and borage, bring to the boil, and cook until tender, about 5–6 minutes. Adjust the salt, and serve immediately, sprinkled with the cheese.

BRUSCANDOLI/BRUSCANSI

HOP SHOOTS *Humulus lupulus*

Although most people know that hop flowers are used in the making

of beer, few are aware in Britain that the fresh shoots can be eaten as a vegetable. The hop is a perennial climber, and grows wild around North America, Europe and in the south of England, particularly in Kent (where Flemish beer-makers introduced the plant in the sixteenth century), climbing its way up garden trellises and telephone poles, sometimes to a height of 3–6m (20–30 ft). It's good in the garden too, as it is fast-growing, providing good cover and decorative flowers. The plant belongs to the Cannabaceae, so a close relative is the hemp which produces marijuana and cannabis!

The shoots, which appear in spring, were eaten as a vegetable and salad in Ancient Rome, according to Pliny, and are still popular all across Europe. In Italy, *bruscandoli* or *bruscansi* (occasionally *punte di luppolo*) are sold in bunches in markets, eaten in a risotto which is a speciality of the Veneto, or simply boiled and sautéed with garlic. *Jets de houblon* are cooked and eaten like very thin asparagus in France and elsewhere, dipped into melted butter or hollandaise sauce. The shoots are also used in soups, salads and omelettes – and the Belgians, who make most use of hop shoots as a vegetable (and, coincidentally, brew quite a lot of hop-flavoured beer as well!), coat them with sauces made from cream and eggs.

The Latin names come from *humus*, earth, and *lupus*, wolf, the latter presumably referring to the plant's habit of strangling its host. The English name is less fanciful, coming from the Anglo-Saxon *hoppan*, to climb. The cone-shaped female flowers of the hop vine, which appear from August to September, contain lupulin, a bitter resin. It is this that is valued in beer-making as flavouring and preservative. (Lupulin is also a calmant, helping you sleep, thus the hop pillows recommended by herbalists.) Hop leaves – large, heart-shaped and deeply indented – are used in France to wrap fresh cheeses, preserving and flavouring them.

RISOTTO DI BRUSCANDOLI

WILD HOP RISOTTO

This recipe is dedicated to Venice where I discovered, at the Rialto daily market, that they sold *bruscandoli*, the tops of wild hops. These are collected on the islands of the *laguna*.

SERVES 4

250g (9 oz) hop tops

1.5 litres (2¾ pints) well seasoned chicken stock

1 small onion, finely chopped

1 garlic clove, finely chopped

75g (2¾ oz) unsalted butter

375g (13 oz) carnaroli rice

55g (2 oz) Parmesan cheese, freshly grated

salt and pepper to taste

Wash the hop tops, and cut into 5cm (2 in) pieces.

The most important element in making risotto is to keep a pot of boiling stock next to the risotto pan. This is necessary because you want to be able to add liquid at the same temperature as the rice to avoid interrupting the cooking. Heat the stock to a simmer.

Start by frying the onion and garlic in 55g (2 oz) of the butter. Add the rice, stirring to coat every grain with the butter. Start to add the hot stock, ladle by ladle, stirring occasionally. After 10 minutes add the hops, which should cook for approximately 8 minutes, or continue until the risotto is creamy and the rice *al dente*. Remove from the heat, add the rest of the butter and the Parmesan, and adjust the seasoning. Serve immediately.

FRITTATA DI BRUSCANDOLI

HOP OMELETTE

To ensure a constant supply of hop shoots, I decided to grow a few plants in my vegetable garden, and they are a joy when in season.

SERVES 4

200g (7 oz) hop shoots

4 tbsp good olive oil

5 large eggs

20g (¾ oz) Parmesan cheese, freshly grated

salt and pepper to taste

Wash the hop shoots and drain well. Pour the oil into an old seasoned frying pan of about 20cm (8 in) in diameter (or a non-stick pan), and heat. Add the hop shoots to the oil, frying gently until they soften, a few minutes only. Beat the eggs, then add the Parmesan and salt and pepper to taste. Pour into the frying pan, and raise the heat slightly to fry one side of the omelette to golden brown. Turn over – by inverting the omelette on to a plate, then back into the frying pan – and fry the second side until golden. Serve warm or cold, cut into wedges.

ACETOSA

SORREL *Rumex acetosa*

Rumex acetosa, common sorrel or garden sorrel, is the wild ancestor of the sorrel we all know from the bundles in good food shops. The latter is usually *R. scutatus*, or French sorrel, which was introduced to Britain from France in the sixteenth century. It has become more popular because it has larger leaves and it is less bitter than *R. acetosa*. For all the sorrels are bitter, because of their oxalic acid content. The plant's names reflect this throughout Europe: *acetosa* or *erba brusca* ('sour grass') in Italy, *Sauerampfer* in Germany, *acedera* in Spain. The English name 'sorrel' comes from the Old French *surele*, or *sur*, 'sour', and a host of local names in English are similar to the commonest, 'sour dabs'.

A perennial, sorrel is easy to recognise. It grows in fields and waste land; the leaves can be picked from February, when they are young and tender, and the little red and green flowers appear from May to August. The thin arrow-shaped leaves of *R. acetosa* (*R. scutatus*, as its Latin name suggests, has shield-shaped leaves), are distributed along a long thin stem, green at first and then colouring faintly red. The plant can reach a height of 70–100cm (30–40 in).

Sorrel is interesting to cook with because of its distinctive sour taste, and it can be puréed with other greens like spinach, made into a soup or fritters, as well as added to omelettes and, my favourite, risottos. It makes wonderful sauces, and was a particularly popular

ingredient of the English 'green sauce' eaten from medieval times with roast and cold meats and fish. Sorrel is also eaten raw in salads, to which its sourness lends a refreshing note. In fact I remember as children we used to chew the juicy, tender part of the stem when we were thirsty.

Because of its oxalic acid content, sorrel should not be eaten too frequently by anyone, but particularly not by those suffering from a number of complaints – kidney trouble, gout and rheumatism among them.

Always cook sorrel in stainless-steel or non-stick pans, as the acid reacts with iron. In fact, the acid content is so high that in Lapland sorrel is used to sour milk instead of rennet.

CREMA DI ACETOSA CON BRUSCHETTA

CREAM OF WILD SORREL SOUP WITH GARLIC CROÛTONS

A delightful soup, which makes an elegant starter at a dinner party. Needless to say, you may use cultivated sorrel instead of wild, but it will be much less satisfying!

SERVES 4

150g (5½ oz) fresh wild sorrel
1 small onion, finely chopped
1 celery stick, finely chopped
1 medium potato, about 200g (7 oz), peeled and cubed
25g (1 oz) unsalted butter
55g (2 oz) mascarpone cheese
40g (1½ oz) Parmesan cheese, freshly grated
salt and pepper to taste

Garlic croûtons
2 large slices country-style bread (quite dense in texture)
1 garlic clove, peeled
55g (2 oz) unsalted butter

Wash the sorrel, and remove any tough stalks. Coarsely chop the leaves.

Fry the onion, celery and potato in the butter for approximately 5 minutes. Add enough water to cover, about 1 litre (1¾ pints), along with some salt, and bring to the boil. After cooking for 8 minutes, add the sorrel and cook for a further 6 minutes. Leave to cool a little, then liquidise in a food processor. It will be thick.

Toast the slices of bread until golden, then rub a little of the garlic on both sides of the toast. Cut into cubes, then fry in the butter until crisp.

Put the liquidised soup into a pan to warm through, then add the mascarpone, stirring well. Season to taste. Serve hot with the croûtons and Parmesan sprinkled on top.

verdure

RISOTTO CON GAMBERI E ACETOSA

WILD SORREL AND PRAWN RISOTTO

I first cooked this risotto a few years ago whilst filming my television series in northern Italy. I called it 'Sophiesticated Risotto' in honour of my niece Sophie on the occasion of her wedding, which I could not attend. The little prawns add taste, texture and colour to the dish.

SERVES 4

150g (5½ oz) wild sorrel leaves

1.5 litres (2¾ pints) well seasoned chicken or
    vegetable stock

3 tbsp extra virgin olive oil

55g (2 oz) unsalted butter

1 small onion, finely chopped

375g (13 oz) carnaroli rice

200g (7 oz) cooked peeled prawns

55g (2 oz) Parmesan cheese, freshly grated

salt and pepper to taste

Wash the sorrel well, then remove any tough stalks. Chop the leaves roughly.

Keep the stock on the boil next to the risotto pan. Add the oil, 40g (1½ oz) of the butter and the onion to the risotto pan, and fry until the onion becomes transparent. Add the rice and stir to coat every grain with the fat. Ladle by ladle, add the hot stock to the rice, stirring until the rice has absorbed all of the liquid. After approximately 10 minutes, add most of the sorrel and cook for 8 minutes, by which time the risotto will have turned slightly green. Next add the prawns, the rest of the butter and the cheese, stirring to form a creamy consistency. Season to taste, scatter with the remaining sorrel, and serve immediately.

CAVOLO MARINO

SEA KALE *Cramba maritima*

Sea kale is a crucifer, a member of the cabbage family, which is reflected in its Italian name, *cavolo marino*, and French names, *chou marin* and *chou de mer*. It grows wild around the shores of Europe, in sand or shingle just above the tide-line, but is not related to seakale beet, which is a chard. I have often watched the indifference (or ignorance) of people walking along shingle beaches in the south of England. Clusters of delicious sea kale were all around, but no-one was paying any attention to or touching them. Sea kale plants can form quite large clumps which, when flowering, slightly resemble loose cauliflower or broccoli heads. At this late stage, the plant is too bitter to be eaten, but what gourmets and wild-food seekers have done for generations is to 'blanch' the plant; as the shoots appear, sand and/or pebbles are heaped around them so that they grow in darkness. This elongates the flowering stems – the edible part – and softens the bitterness of the flavour (the same process as is applied to many plants in the chicory family).

The blanched broccoli-like tops, which are a cluster of unopened buds, are cooked and eaten as asparagus, with melted butter or other butter sauces. They can also be cooked in a cheese sauce in the oven. Use the tender top leaves as well.

CAVOLO MARINO ALL'AGLIO E PEPERONCINO

SEA KALE WITH GARLIC AND CHILLI

Use the broccoli-like spears and tender top leaves for this dish, which can be eaten alone or with lamb cutlets or bread.

SERVES 4

800g (1¾ lb) fresh sea kale tops
6 tbsp extra virgin olive oil
2 garlic cloves, finely chopped
1 chilli, finely chopped
salt to taste

Cook the sea kale in slightly salted water until *al dente*, about 4–5 minutes depending on size. Heat the oil in a pan and add the garlic and chilli, frying briefly. Drain the kale, and serve hot with the flavoured oil poured over the top.

CAVOLO MARINO AL BURRO E PARMIGIANO

SEA KALE WITH BUTTER AND PARMESAN

The combination of butter and Parmesan is perfect with a huge variety of vegetables, whether cultivated or wild. It's best with the freshest ingredients, though.

Serve this dish as a starter, or to accompany fish dishes or pale meats such as veal, chicken or rabbit.

SERVES 4

800g (1¾ lb) fresh sea kale tops (see above)
85g (3 oz) unsalted butter, melted
85g (3 oz) Parmesan cheese, freshly grated
salt and pepper to taste

Put the sea kale into boiling salted water and cook for 4–5 minutes, depending on size. Drain and transfer to a hot plate. Pour the butter over the top, then sprinkle with the cheese. Season to taste, and serve immediately.

verdure

CARDONE SELVATICO

MARSH THISTLE *Cirsium palustre*

This is my latest wild food discovery, although I already knew that many European thistles – some of them members of the cardoon and artichoke family – were edible. There are over ten distinct wild thistles in the British Isles alone, of which four have completely prickly stems. Marsh thistle is one of them, and as the stem is the edible part, you have to be very careful when cutting and preparing the plant!

Marsh thistle is common throughout Europe, growing in grassy fields, in woodland clearings, at roadsides and obviously, because of its name, in marshes, as it favours wet ground. It can grow from 60cm–1.8m (2–6 ft) in height; it has prickly leaves off a straight, very prickly stem, topped with a thistle head of pale pink tufts. You will find it from April to August; the best time to cut the stems to eat is between June and July, preferably before the flower appears.

I first encountered marsh thistle in the damp field next to our house in the country, where it was very tenacious, resisting many attempts to get rid of it. My revenge was to cut and cook it – but I have to report that it is now growing back stronger than ever, and faster than we can eat it! I cut off the top of the plant, about 13cm (5 in), then remove the spiky leaves, and the tough spiny skin of the stem. The stem centre remaining is pale green and very juicy. The stems can be eaten raw – they are nutty and fresh, and are good as part of mixed salads or crudités – but are delicious when boiled and eaten as a vegetable. They are often called 'poor man's asparagus', as they can be eaten in a similar way.

verdure

CARDONE AL BURRO E PARMIGIANO

MARSH THISTLE WITH BUTTER AND PARMESAN

Serve this dish on its own, as a starter perhaps, or as a vegetable accompaniment.

SERVES 4

600g (1 lb 5 oz) marsh thistle stems, prepared

55g (2 oz) unsalted butter, melted

55g (2 oz) Parmesan cheese, freshly grated

salt to taste

Put the spears into boiling salted water and cook for 5–6 minutes. Drain and place on a hot plate. Pour the melted butter over the top, and sprinkle with the Parmesan.

PINZIMONIO

ITALIAN CRUDITÉS

It is a Tuscan and Roman custom to taste the first fresh vegetable of the season, raw and dipped into extra virgin olive oil from the last olive harvest. These vegetables, accompanied by bread, make an ideal starter for a springtime or early summer meal. Marsh thistles are only one amongst a long list of vegetables that can be used similarly, such as spring onions, fennel, radishes and so on.

SERVES 4

20 marsh thistle stems, peeled

8 asparagus spears, peeled

20 spring onions, cleaned

20 radishes, trimmed

4 small fennel bulbs, inside part only, quartered

200ml (7 fl oz) extra virgin olive oil

coarse sea salt

coarsely ground black pepper

12 small pieces *bruschetta, crostini* or bread

Put all the vegetables in a bowl with water and ice. Prepare little individual bowls with the olive oil, in which you put some salt and pepper to taste.

Dip 1 piece of vegetable at a time into the oil, stirring a little to catch some of the salt and pepper at the bottom of the bowl. Eat with the bread.

SALICORNIA

MARSH SAMPHIRE *Salicornia europaea*

Samphire, a plant which readily colonises tidal marshes and mudflats, is one of the best wild green vegetables. It is found all round coastal Britain – most commonly in East Anglia – and in Europe. Not to be confused with rock samphire (a cliff-growing wild vegetable plant related to the goosefoot family, Chenopodiaceae), marsh samphire looks like a cross between a succulent and a seaweed, with a cluster of green, jointed stems, the plump flesh of which forms the leaves. The plant is annual, grows up to 20–40cm (8–16 in) in height, and becomes red-yellow as it matures. To be at its best, samphire should be washed by the tide, and traditionally should not be picked until after the longest day. It is available in Britain in July and August: in July the juicy shoots will be very tender; by September they will be succulent and fat. It is found in fishmongers usually, rather than greengrocers, not only because it accompanies fish so well, but because it is usually gathered by fishermen and their wives. Stocks of samphire at other times throughout the year come from France, where it is known as *salade de mer*, *passe-pierre* or *salicorne*. In Italy *salicornia* is not used much apart from in the Veneto, where it grows abundantly. It is mixed into salads as a piquant ingredient.

If you want to pick some from the wild, check first that you are not trespassing! Arm yourself with a bucket and some high, waterproof boots, and don't be afraid of mud. Cut the plant just above the root (never pull out by the roots), and wash very well at home. Don't keep it in water or it will quickly decay. If you want to keep it for a few days, do so in the fridge, but as dry as possible. To cook, boil briefly (without salt as it is salty enough already), then serve with melted butter or warmed olive oil. Pick a stem up by the root end and bite lightly, scraping the flesh away from the stringy centre with your teeth. Samphire can also be pickled.

An alternative name for marsh samphire in Britain is glasswort. The plant is rich in soda salts, so was once used in the soap and glass industries.

SALICORNIA SOTT'ACETO

PICKLED SAMPHIRE

Preserving has always been used to keep food collected from a bumper crop for a longer time, to enable it to be enjoyed out of season. Depending on the items to be preserved, sugar, salt, vinegar or alcohol can be the means of halting the natural deterioration. However, in the process the taste and texture of the original items can change dramatically, to produce a completely new range of foods, each containing different characteristics. Pickled, samphire becomes an interesting accompaniment to meat or fish or as an *antipasto*.

FILLS A 1KG (2¼ LB) JAR

600g (1 lb 5 oz) fresh samphire

500ml (18 fl oz) strong white wine vinegar

100g (3½ oz) caster sugar

a few bay leaves

a few sprigs of fresh dill

1 tbsp juniper berries

Wash the samphire well in several changes of cold water.

In a large pan, bring the vinegar, sugar and herb and spice flavourings to the boil. Add the samphire and cook for 10 minutes. (Salt is not needed because samphire is very salty indeed.) Remove from the heat, leave to cool, and bottle in a clean airtight jar. You can use it straightaway.

CICORIA DI CAMPO

DANDELION *Taraxacum officinale*

This garden weed must be one of the most common of the wild greens, and it is widely distributed and eaten throughout the northern hemisphere. The English name derives from the French *dent-de-lion*, or lion's tooth. The Italians also call it *dente di leone*, as well as *cicoria di campo* (field chicory), which makes sense as dandelion's nearest edible relative is actually wild chicory. However, the most frequent local name in many countries refers to the plant's diuretic properties, long known in herbal medicine (and still recognised today). In France, the plant is known as *pissenlit*, in Italy *pissialetto*, and in the UK as 'pissabed' or 'wetabed'.

I remember my mother's insistence on our collecting as many of these healthy leaves as possible in spring (as I can also remember an aching back, and hands black from the milky juices of the dandelion stems). She served the leaves raw in salads (see page 31) with other greens, braised them with capers, chilli and garlic, or with beans, or boiled them (which lessens the bitterness) to use as a filling in vegetable tarts.

Although it is obviously the leaves that are most widely eaten, other parts of the plant are used as well. Properly dried, roasted and ground, the roots make a coffee substitute which is caffeine-free; this was particularly common in England during the Second World War when real coffee was unavailable. In Italy still, a coffee made from toasted dandelion roots (or *orzo,* barley) is drunk by children. The flower buds can be pickled to substitute for capers, and the brilliant yellow flowers are often used in Europe to make dandelion wine and dandelion beers, or deep-fried in a batter as fritters.

Dandelions are a very hardy plant, and will survive frosts. They begin to grow once the coldest weather is past, and the tender young leaves were valued because they were one of the first greens available in spring. In cultivation, dandelion plants can be blanched (kept away from the light), which also reduces bitterness (as for other members of the chicory family).

TORTA DI CICORIA

DANDELION PIE

This recipe is derived from *pizza di scarola*, a popular peasant dish in the south of Italy, where farmers use big bunches of dandelion plus a few other humble ingredients to produce the most delightful pie. The large dandelion leaves of early summer have a slightly bitter taste, which is ideal for this dish.

SERVES 4

300g (10½ oz) Italian soft wheat 00 flour
200g (7 oz) lard or unsalted butter,
    at room temperature, cut into small cubes
a pinch of salt
water as required
1 egg yolk for glazing

Filling

700g (1 lb 9oz) dandelion leaves, washed and
    roughly chopped
6 tbsp extra virgin olive oil
3 garlic cloves, finely chopped
1 tbsp salted capers, prepared (see page 139)
1 fresh chilli, finely chopped
55g (2 oz) green or black pitted olives
2 tbsp raisins
2 tbsp pine kernels
4 anchovy fillets, roughly chopped

For the pastry, mix the flour with the lard or butter, salt and enough water – about 6 tbsp – to produce a pliable dough. Knead it well, then cover and let it rest in the fridge for 20–30 minutes.

For the filling, blanch the dandelion leaves in slightly salted water for 15–20 minutes. Drain and squeeze out excess liquid. Put the olive oil into a large pan and add the garlic, capers, chilli and olives, and fry briefly. Add the dandelion leaves, raisins, pine kernels and anchovies, and stir-fry until the anchovies are cooked.

Meanwhile, preheat the oven to 200°C/400°F/Gas 6.

Grease a tart ring of about 25cm (10 in) in diameter with a little extra lard. Roll half the pastry out to 3mm (⅛ in) thickness, and then transfer to the tart ring, trimming off any excess. Roll out the rest of the pastry to a circle of the same size. Fill the ring with the filling mixture, and then cover with the circle of pastry to form a lid. Seal by pinching the dough together around the rim. Pierce a hole in the top to let the steam out. Brush with egg yolk, then bake in the preheated oven for 25–30 minutes. Serve hot or cold.

INSALATA PRIMAVERILE

SPRINGTIME SALAD

Springtime, when all the tender, new-grown greens such as dandelion, wild garlic and sorrel appear, marks the beginning of my wild salad leaf season. Later on, in early summer, you can add wild fennel, wild rocket and mint, and I usually decorate my salads with some flowers such as violets or primroses. You could add some cultivated spring onion for added flavour if you like.

This salad is an essential dish for Easter Monday picnics in Italy, as is the hop shoot omelette on page 16, and a traditional Easter cake, *pastiera di grano.*

SERVES 4

350g (12 oz) mixed spring leaves

a few flower heads and petals (violets, primrose,

dandelion, borage)

4 large eggs

3 tbsp good olive oil (extra virgin preferably)

1 tbsp wine vinegar

12 anchovy fillets in oil

salt and pepper to taste

Briefly wash the salad leaves and flowers, and drain very well. Hard-boil the eggs, but not *too* hard, as they are much nicer this way. Shell them, and cut in half.

Mix the oil and vinegar together to make a vinaigrette, adding salt and pepper to taste. Toss the salad leaves with this in a large bowl, and garnish with the egg halves, anchovies and flowers. Eat with a good home-made bread, preferably wholegrain.

verdure

CENOPODIO

FAT HEN *Chenopodium album*

It was only late in life that I started to appreciate the potential culinary uses of this wild plant, known as *cenopodio* or *Buon Enrico* in Italy, and often as the equivalent of the latter, Good King Henry, in the UK. Its grey-green leaves, which are always juicy and cool to the touch, are shaped like an arrowhead, or the webbed foot of a goose – the generic name *Chenopodium* actually coming from the Greek for 'goose foot'. In fact, fat hen is an important member of the goosefoot family, which includes the oraches (cultivated relatives are spinach and sugar beet). They are possibly the best wild leaves for eating, with a flavour reminiscent of kale and young broccoli. Use the leaves and tender tops, discarding the tougher stalks.

Fat hen likes to grow on waste ground and around farmyards, thus its local English names of dungweed, muckweed, even dirty dick! It grows abundantly between the rows of plants in my country vegetable garden. The fact that it is a plant loved by birds is reflected elsewhere in Europe, not least in 'fat hen' itself: in France it is *grasse poulette*, in German, *Fette Henne* (although it is known as pigweed in the USA). The plants, which can grow up to 1m (3 ft) in height, are commonly cultivated in Greece and elsewhere as a vegetable. The greenish flowers, which appear from May to August, can be eaten as well when still in small, tight bunches. The seeds were used by American Indians to make flour, and Napoleon is said to have existed for a while on a dark bread made from fat hen seeds. The flour tastes rather like buckwheat, so would make good galettes and pancakes.

Interestingly, quinoa, the South American grain, has been developed from close relatives of fat hen. And fat hen has been eaten, leaves and seeds, as food since neolithic times: the contents of the stomach of 'Tollund man', a Stone Age man perfectly preserved by the tannic acids of a peat bog in Denmark, included barley, linseed, fat hen seeds and sorrel. It's not surprising he ate fat hen, for the leaves are said to contain more iron and protein than spinach, and more vitamin B and calcium than raw cabbage. Cook as spinach.

verdure

CREMA DI CENOPODIO

CREAM OF FAT HEN SOUP

This soup reminds me of my good friend Nina Burgai in the Aosta Valley. She is the owner of a hotel which is at 6,000 feet, and it is very easy for her to pick all sorts of greens to be used in a creamed soup.

SERVES 4

600g (1 lb 5 oz) fat hen (or you can use a mixture – borage, dandelion, nettle, sorrel, wild garlic, rocket), chopped
55g (2 oz) unsalted butter
3 garlic cloves, finely chopped
1 medium onion, finely chopped
1 large carrot, cubed
2 large potatoes, cubed

2 tbsp chopped fresh parsley
800ml (28 fl oz) chicken stock
salt and pepper to taste

Saffron croûtons

1 sachet saffron powder or strands
40g (1½ oz) unsalted butter
3 slices white bread, cubed

Melt the butter in a large pan and stir-fry the garlic, onion, carrot, potatoes and parsley for a few minutes, then add the stock and cook until the potatoes and carrots are soft, about 10 minutes. Add the greens, then cook for a further 10 minutes. Season to taste, cool a little and then blend in a food processor until creamy. Return to the pan.

If using saffron strands to make the croûtons, toast them first. Put them on a metal spoon and 'toast' them over a flame to dry them. Then crumble them. Put the butter, saffron and bread cubes into a pan and fry until crisp. Serve the soup hot, sprinkled with the croûtons.

CENOPODIO AL PARMIGIANO

FAT HEN WITH PARMESAN

The pleasure I gain from this recipe is immense, especially considering its simplicity. It may be eaten as a delicate starter or a side dish.

SERVES 4

600g (1 lb 5 oz) fat hen leaves, washed
55g (2 oz) unsalted butter
juice of ¼ lemon

55g (2 oz) Parmesan cheese
salt and pepper to taste

Plunge the leaves into boiling, salted water and cook for exactly 1 minute. Drain, and then return to the pan immediately. Add the butter, lemon juice, salt and pepper and mix well. Transfer to warm plates, and then grate the Parmesan directly on top.

VALERIANELLA

LAMB'S LETTUCE/CORN SALAD *Valerianella locusta*

Corn salad or lamb's lettuce is an annual member of the valerian
family – it's known as *valerianella* in Italy – and is native to Europe, North Africa and the
Middle East, growing on roadsides, arable land, in gardens (where it is considered a weed),
and even in cracks in walls. It has grown wild in Europe since at least the sixteenth century
– John Evelyn, the English diarist, recommended the use of 'corn-sallet' in spring and autumn
salads in 1699. Today a cultivated variety is very popular in France – where it is most
commonly known as *mâche* or *doucette* – Germany and the United States. The plant consists
of oval, pale green leaves some 5cm (2 in) long, which grow from a very small root into a
cluster of about 10cm (4 in) high. It can be sown successively throughout the year. An Italian
corn salad, *V. eriocarpa*, grows only in the Mediterranean area, and has longer, paler leaves.

The leaves are very tender and delicate – tasting nutty at their best – and are delicious in
salads. These I would dress in the Italian way, adding olive oil first to coat the leaves, to
protect them from the acidity of the lemon juice or vinegar. Corn salad can also be cooked
like spinach. *Sarzet,* as the leaf was known in the part of Italy I come from, was a frequent
ingredient in our springtime daily salad. Armed with a knife and basket I would collect it
in the vineyards, between the rows of vines, or from fruit orchards or fields lying fallow
from the previous year. (If collecting from vineyards or orchards, be careful that the plants
have not been sprayed with pesticides.)

VALERIANELLA (CON ACETO DI LAMPONE)

LAMB'S LETTUCE WITH RASPBERRY VINAIGRETTE

Provided that you collect only the most tender leaves, this salad may be used to accompany pale meats, especially something like a Milanese cutlet, or fish. The fragrance of a little raspberry vinegar with some olive oil makes it quite a delicacy.

SERVES 4

300g (10½ oz) lamb's lettuce

4 large tbsp extra virgin olive oil

1 tbsp *Raspberry Vinegar* (see below)

salt and pepper to taste

Clean the lamb's lettuce carefully. Pour the oil over the leaves, then mix to coat thoroughly. Add some salt and pepper and then the vinegar. If you add the vinegar last, the leaves will remain crisp, and the flavour will be mellower. Serve immediately.

ACETO DI LAMPONE

RASPBERRY VINEGAR

While preparing food for photography with my invaluable assistant, Kate Habershon, I wanted to make some raspberry vinegar. Kate had a recipe, which I've used, but I've modified the sugar slightly, as I like the vinegar to be less sweet. Use the vinegar in vinaigrettes, in game dishes, in fruit salads and in drinks.

MAKES 1 LITRE (1¾ PINTS)

500g (18 oz) ripe wild raspberries

600ml (1 pint) good white wine vinegar

300g (10½ oz) caster sugar

Put the raspberries into the vinegar and leave to macerate for ten days.

Strain the vinegar off, retaining the fruit (for what to do with the latter, see page 63). At this stage the vinegar will have a nice colour. Add the caster sugar, then bring to the boil to melt the sugar. As soon as the liquid is clear, leave it to cool. Bottle in sterilised bottles when cold.

ORTICA

STINGING NETTLE *Urtica dioica*

Although widely regarded nowadays as a garden pest, the stinging nettle has always been valued as food throughout Europe. Indeed the nettle 'follows' man (what is known as a 'culture-follower'), for it flourishes in nitrogen- and phosphate-rich soil, and man, with his animals, his middens, waste grounds and graveyards, provides a plentiful supply of these plant nutrients. Some 'lost' villages and houses have actually been rediscovered because of the give-away growths of nettles on the site.

The plant is perennial, and grows anywhere throughout most of the year, unless there is a severe frost or snow. The leaves, which are covered in stinging hairs, are dark green and heart shaped. The hairs also cover the plant stems, and they contain formic acid (the same as that in ant bites). The edible parts are the tops of the young shoots, which appear in spring, and no less an expert than Aristophanes said that nettles should be cooked and eaten before the annual arrival of the swallows. Most of the leaves become coarser and more bitter in flavour after June, although the top leaves can still be eaten – but avoid the flowers.

Nettle leaves are almost always cooked – which destroys the sting – but can occasionally be used in salads. Pick them with care, always wearing sturdy gloves. (If you want to impress your friends, make them think you are oblivious to nettle stings. All the stinging hairs on the leaves and stems point upwards, so approach the plant from the bottom rather than the top, and you won't get stung!) Nettles make good purées, sauces, soups, tarts and soufflés in much the same way as spinach. In Italy they are used in omelettes and risottos and, again instead of spinach, in ravioli fillings and to make a green pasta. In the north of England an Easter 'pudding' used to be made using the first greens of spring, often easterledge, dock or nettle, and nettles made a beer very similar to ginger beer. Nettle juice, rather like that of sorrel, has been used as a vegetarian substitute for rennet, to curdle milk.

verdure

TORTA DI ORTICHE

NETTLE TART

Why use nettles, when this dish could easily be made with any other type of greens? The reason is that nettles, whilst probably being the most scorned vegetable on earth, also have a delightful nutty taste, contain lots of natural goodness, and on top of that, they cost nothing. Be careful to wear gloves when collecting, and if you then put the nettles in a plastic bag in the fridge before preparation, it reduces their sting!

SERVES 4

350g (12 oz) nettle leaves

12 quails' eggs

20g (¾ oz) lard, melted

10 sheets filo pastry

4 medium eggs, beaten

150g (5½ oz) Parmesan or Cheddar cheese, freshly grated

½ tsp freshly grated nutmeg

15g (½ oz) dry fine breadcrumbs

15g (½ oz) unsalted butter

salt and pepper to taste

Preheat the oven to 200°C/400°F/Gas 6.

Cook the cleaned nettle leaves in salted water for 5–8 minutes, depending on their toughness. Strain and squeeze out the excess water. Leave to cool and then chop roughly. Cook the quails' eggs for approximately 7–8 minutes, then cool and remove their shells.

Brush a round baking tin of 25cm (10 in) in diameter and 5cm (2 in) high with a little lard, then place a sheet of filo pastry on the base. Brush with lard, and then continue to layer the sheets one by one, overlapping slightly, until the whole inside of the tin is covered.

Mix the chopped nettle leaves in a bowl with the beaten eggs, cheese, nutmeg and salt and pepper to taste. Place the quails' eggs on the filo pastry, then cover with the nettle mixture to fill the tin. Trim any excess filo pastry from around the edge of the tin, leaving 2.5cm (1 in) overlapping. Fold the pastry over the filling, taking care to leave the middle uncovered. Sprinkle the tart with the breadcrumbs and small dabs of the butter. Bake for 15 minutes in the preheated oven until golden brown. Serve hot in wedges.

verdure

NETTLE GNOCCHI WITH DOLCELATTE SAUCE

Gnocchi are one of the most satisfying dishes of Italian cuisine. The name, which translates to 'dumplings' in English (and is very difficult for foreigners to pronounce!), is probably derived from the Germanic food culture – from the *Knödeln* and *Nockerln* of Germany and Austria. Including nettles in the mix not only gives a nice colour, but also a nutty taste.

SERVES 4

200g (7 oz) nettle leaves

700g (1 lb 9 oz) floury potatoes, peeled and cubed

200g (7 oz) plain flour, plus a little extra for dusting

1 large egg

salt and pepper to taste

Dolcelatte sauce

100g (3½ oz) dolcelatte cheese, cut into small cubes

100ml (3½ fl oz) milk

55g (2 oz) unsalted butter

To serve

55g (2 oz) Parmesan cheese, freshly grated

Cook the nettles in boiling salted water for 10 minutes, then drain and squeeze out all the residual liquid. Cook the potatoes in boiling salted water until tender, then drain and mash to a purée while still warm.

Put the potatoes on a clean work surface and mix in the flour. Liquidise the nettles with the egg, and season to taste. Add this to the potato mixture, and knead to a soft dough.

On a well-floured surface, take sections of dough at a time and roll them out with the palm of your hand to form a sausage 2cm (¾ in) in diameter. Cut into chunks of about 3cm (1¼ in) in length, and dust with a little flour. Continue this way until all the mixture is finished. Using a well-floured fork, take a piece at a time and roll it down over the prongs, to form a pattern that resembles little ridged shells as they fall off the fork. Leave to rest on a clean cloth.

Next, combine the dolcelatte and milk and process together. Melt the butter in a large pan, then add the milk and cheese, and allow to melt over a low heat.

Bring a large pot of salted water to the boil, then add the *gnocchi*. When they rise to the surface after a few seconds, they are ready. Drain them and add to the sauce immediately. Sprinkle with the Parmesan and some black pepper. Serve hot.

verdure

RUCHETTA/RUCOLA

ROCKET *Eruca sativa*

One of my daily culinary duties as a child was collecting a small bunch of fresh wild rocket for our daily salad in the spring and summer. This I did on returning home from school for lunch, and where I collected could not have been closer to home – along the railway tracks! For rocket seems to grow as happily in waste places, in poor soil, as it does in the herb garden. That rocket likes the quality soil of the latter is proved by the fact that you can have leaves ready in from six to eight weeks from sowing! It is a very fast-growing plant.

Wild rocket grows as a small bush, up to 30–60cm (1–2 ft) high, and is native to Asia and the Mediterranean. The dandelion-like leaves, which are very coarsely lobed, are strong in taste, between mustard and watercress, revealing the plant's membership of the crucifer or cabbage family, along with other peppery plants such as mustard, cress and radish. The plant produces very delicate creamy-yellow flowers from February to October, which can be used in salads along with the leaves. In Italy, we distinguish between *ruchetta*, the wild rocket, and *rucola*, the cultivated version. The latter, which has larger leaves, cannot compare in flavour to the former. In America, the plant is known by yet another Italian name, *arugula*. In Italian cooking, the use of rocket has been extended and now encompasses pasta sauces (there is even a rocket pesto), inclusion in risottos and sandwiches, and it is also used as a tasty garnish for *carpaccio* (thinly sliced raw beef).

SALSA DI RUCHETTA

WILD ROCKET SALSA

I specifically created this recipe to accompany the *Parcel of Crab* recipe on page 162. It is equally useful as an accompaniment to grilled meat or fish. I like it on *crostini* with mozzarella and tomato, and it can also be used as a pesto with some basil to flavour hot pasta dishes and cold pasta salads.

SERVES 6–8

150g (5½ oz) rocket leaves, washed

8 tbsp extra virgin olive oil

2 tbsp white wine vinegar or lemon juice

1 garlic clove, finely chopped

1 tsp salt

1 tsp caster sugar

2 tbsp chopped fresh flat-leaf parsley

Blend all the ingredients together in a food processor to obtain a smooth sauce. The flavour of the *salsa* is quite powerful and slightly bitter due to the natural bitterness of the rocket.

CARNE ALL'ALBESE

BEEF ALBA STYLE

Rocket's mustardy, slightly bitter flavour livens up many salads and other foods which might otherwise be bland. Rocket is an essential accompaniment to *carpaccio*, the famous raw beef dish which originated in the legendary Harry's Bar in Venice. *Carpaccio* is also eaten a lot in Alba in Piedmont where, with a topping of thinly sliced truffles, the dish is known as meat *all'albese*, 'Alba style'. In the absence of truffle, you can use slivers of Parmesan as here, and a few drops of truffle oil.

SERVES 4

a good bunch of fresh rocket

500g (18 oz) very lean fillet of beef in the piece

4 tbsp good olive oil

juice of 1 lemon

55g (2 oz) Parmesan cheese in the piece

salt and pepper to taste

Wash and drain the rocket leaves. Cut the beef into 12 very thin slices. Put each slice of beef between 2 pieces of clingfilm, and beat them even thinner with a meat bat or wooden mallet, taking care not to tear them.

Cover each of 4 large plates with 3 of the beef slices. Spread over these evenly a quarter each of the olive oil and lemon juice, and season with salt and pepper to taste. Cut very thin slices of Parmesan and distribute them between the plates. Top generously with the rocket, and serve with a good country bread.

erbe

HERBS

AT ONE TIME HERBS AND SPICES WERE USED IN COOKING TO CAMOUFLAGE THE taste of bad meat or fish. What a waste! For to me herbs are the soul of cooking. They are used to enhance the flavour of particular ingredients, and to impart a very distinctive identity to individual dishes. In many cases the combination of two or three herbal flavours make a famous and complementary marriage. Think of oven-roasted potatoes with garlic and rosemary; fennel with fish; mint with meat or eel, or in sauces; horseradish with beef. Sometimes a single herb or a combination can encapsulate a cooking style, represent the essence of a cuisine: cooking with oregano, mint and garlic (although not necessarily together) gives a Mediterranean flavour to a dish, whilst using coriander and lemongrass reminds one of Thailand.

To be able to appreciate wonderful flavours in a dish, whether of herbs or not, one has to have good taste-buds. Our 'taste memory' is almost infallible, and stays with us throughout our lives. How many times have you tasted something, and it was instantly familiar, actually reminding you of your first meeting, a particular occasion, circumstance or place? To me taste is as evocative in that sense as smell. It is also wonderful to discover new tastes and flavours which, if accepted by your palate and taste-buds, will then be stored in your memory as a pleasant experience.

Herbs have been cultivated for thousands of years. It was the Romans who, as they marched in conquest across Europe, were responsible for the spread of their favourite herbs. For most herbs we use – and which have become familiar further north – are plants of the warmer Mediterranean. Many herbs, cultivated in medieval domestic and monastery gardens as medicines and flavourings, escaped into the wild, and have become familiar plants of the European countryside.

The flavours of these wild plants are much stronger than those that have been cultivated. There is also a big difference between fresh and dried herbs. When dried, rosemary and oregano become stronger in flavour while dried mint becomes milder, due to the loss of its essential oils in the drying process. Basil does not dry well at all (to preserve it, you should freeze it in olive oil). Always try to use herbs fresh, during their season, when they are in their prime. If you have a surplus, you could dry them in small bunches.

In the following pages I have only touched on a few of the endless flavoured plants which you can encounter in the wild.

erbe

AGLIO SELVATICO

RAMSONS (WILD GARLIC) *Allium ursinum*

There are many species of wild garlic, including *Allium triquetrum*, a wild relative of the leek, but ramsons – from the Old English *hramsan*, 'wild garlic' – is probably the most common. Also known as bear's garlic (thus the Latin *ursinum*), the plant grows prolifically in shady, cool and damp places. From a tiny onion bulb grows a flowering stem which can reach up to a height of 45cm (18 in). The flowers, which crown the stem like a cluster of delicate white stars, appear from April until June. The leaves resemble those of lily of the valley, but are a much deeper green in colour. They are most succulent at the beginning of the season, in early spring, becoming quite leathery thereafter. All parts of the plant are aromatic: I use the leaves first, then the flowers, then the stem which remains quite

juicy and very tender after the rest of the plant has withered. I don't use the bulbs because they are small and tough, and you want the plants to keep on growing anyway! One of the surest ways of detecting the presence of wild garlic in any particular location is simply stopping and sniffing. You will smell it!

Besides fungi, the wild ingredient my restaurant clients seem to appreciate most is wild garlic. Its delicate, gentle fragrance can be used with almost anything, and it is inoffensive even to the minority who dislike cultivated garlic. My first attempt to use the leaves of wild garlic was sandwiched between some slices of bread sprinkled with extra virgin olive oil and sea salt – a real delicacy!

erbe

PASTA ALL'AGLIO SELVATICO E SALMONE AFFUMICATO

PASTA WITH WILD GARLIC AND SMOKED SALMON

This is one of those accidental recipes which I invented using what I had left over in the fridge. In fact, to be honest, many of the most successful recipes are created in this way!

SERVES 4

1 bunch wild garlic leaves

450g (1 lb) *Fresh Pasta* (see page 104), or 400g (14 oz)
   dried tagliolini, linguine or other thin pasta

2 tbsp olive oil

1 large egg

55g (2 oz) unsalted butter

1 small onion, finely sliced

200g (7 oz) smoked salmon, cut into small strips

salt and pepper to taste

Wash the garlic leaves, and cut into strips at the last minute. Make the fresh pasta as in the basic recipe on page 104, and cut into thin ribbons. Put aside. Bring a large saucepan of generously salted water to the boil.

Meanwhile, heat the oil in a small frying pan. Beat the egg with a little salt, and fry 2 omelettes as thin as a pancake. Cut these into little strips. Wipe out the pan, then melt the butter, and fry the onion until soft and transparent. Add the omelette strips, and stir a little.

Cook the pasta until *al dente* – 3 minutes if fresh, 7 minutes if dried. Drain well and add to the pan with the onion and egg. Mix and serve immediately on hot plates. Top each portion with a quarter of the wild garlic and the salmon.

erbe

ZUPPA D'AGLIO SELVATICO FROXFIELD

FROXFIELD WILD GARLIC SOUP

Foraging through the pretty lanes around Froxfield, an idyllic spot in the south of England where we have a house, it is possible to collect certain wild edible items, which are ancestors of the produce we now find in markets. One of these is wild garlic, which grows everywhere in the area, and you can certainly appreciate the aroma whilst out walking between March and May. The wonderful luscious green leaves and even the pretty white flowers can be used in many different ways, as an addition to salads, stews or grilled foods. The soup is very easy to make and is a nice way to celebrate springtime.

SERVES 4

18 wild garlic leaves

6 large free-range eggs

55g (2 oz) Parmesan cheese, freshly grated

1.2 litres (2 pints) chicken or vegetable stock

55g (2 oz) unsalted butter, softened

4 large slices brown bread, toasted

salt and pepper to taste

Cut 12 of the wild garlic leaves into small strips, and finely chop the remainder. Beat the eggs with a whisk in a large bowl, and then add the Parmesan and some salt and pepper to taste. Bring the stock to a simmer, and when it is boiling, pour a little at a time on to the egg mixture and whisk immediately, which should result in the egg coagulating to form a thick soup. Ladle into hot bowls and sprinkle the strips of garlic leaves on top. Mix the finely chopped garlic leaves with the softened butter and spread on the toast. Serve this with the soup.

erbe

FOCACCIA ALL'AGLIO SELVATICO

WILD GARLIC *FOCACCIA* BREAD

Focaccia, a relation of the pizza, has taken the British by storm, and is now popular not only in Italian restaurants and delicatessens, but even in supermarkets. For me, the best *focaccia* is always the simplest one, topped with coarse sea salt and extra virgin olive oil. However, this variation made with wild garlic is a delicious meal in itself. Don't be tempted to add too many herbs to it, as simplicity always pays off.

SERVES 10

Focaccia

45g (1½ oz) fresh yeast

700ml (23 fl oz) lukewarm water

85ml (3 fl oz) extra virgin olive oil

30g (1¼ oz) fine salt

1.25kg (2¾ lb) Italian soft wheat 00 flour

300g (10½ oz) fine semolina

Topping

150g (5½ oz) wild garlic leaves and flowers, finely chopped

100ml (3½ fl oz) extra virgin olive oil

100g (3½ oz) shelled almonds, finely crushed

salt and pepper to taste

15g (½ oz) coarse salt

For the *focaccia* itself, dissolve the yeast in a little of the lukewarm water – about 50ml (2 fl oz) – then mix with the olive oil and fine salt. Mix this into the flours to make a dough. Set aside in a warm place and cover with a clean cloth. Leave to rise until doubled in size, about 1 hour.

Meanwhile, prepare the topping by coarsely liquidising the garlic leaves (reserving the flowers if you like), together with the olive oil. Add the almonds, salt and pepper to taste, and mix together.

Preheat the oven to 220°C/425°F/Gas 7.

Take the dough and knead to remove any air bubbles. Spread the dough out on a baking tray of 60 x 40cm (24 x 16 in) greased with olive oil. It should cover the whole tray and not be higher than 2cm (¾ in). With the tips of your fingers make dimples in the surface of the dough. Bake in the preheated oven for 20 minutes.

When brown and crisp, remove from the oven. Spread the wild garlic mixture, the flowers if you like, and the coarse salt on the top. Return to the oven for 2 more minutes. Serve warm or cold – either is delicious.

erbe

ROSMARINO

ROSEMARY *Rosmarinus officinalis*

Rosemary is one of the commonest wild herbs of the Mediterranean, growing in profusion on dry hillsides, but it can flourish further north. Because they loved it so much, the Romans took it through Europe, and it can still be found growing wild in various places, often near the sea (*Rosmarinus* means 'dew of the sea') or, in southern England, in graveyards where it was planted because of its traditional association with remembrance. A perennial shrub, rosemary grows to about 2m (6½ feet) high, and it is often used as a hedge. Its leaves are needle shaped, green above and grey below, and attractive blue flowers appear in July and August in Britain, longer in hotter climates.

The camphor-like pungency of rosemary is most often allied with meat, especially in Italy, where it is much liked. In fact, in some Italian butchers, they give sprigs of herbs to the customers, particularly rosemary, much as fishmongers do with parsley in Britain. Rosemary goes well with pork, veal, lamb and rabbit, and can be burned on the barbecue coals to give a more aromatic savour to the smoke. It can be used in marinades, *bouquets garnis*, or in sauces, but very finely chopped because the leaves are tough. It can flavour aromatic jellies and jams, and sugar (as vanilla). It should be used with some discretion, though, as it is strong. The wild, more southerly plants have a much stronger flavour. Rosemary dries well, but is much better fresh.

Rosemary has been of great value for centuries in herbal medicine, primarily as an antiseptic (the reason it is useful in meat marinades), and is reputed to be good for the memory (students would wear garlands of rosemary to improve their performance).

Wild rosemary always reminds me of the time when I was acting as a financial consultant. I was driving some clients through the narrow roads of Ibiza looking to find investment opportunities for them. I'm afraid it was rather a slow business as I kept having to stop the car to leap out and cut bunches of wild rosemary. My enthusiasm – or perhaps it was the pungency of the rosemary itself – must have had some effect, for the day's trip was ultimately very successful in a financial sense!

erbe

ARISTA DI MAIALE

ROAST PORK WITH ROSEMARY

It is best to use pork on the bone for more flavour, although you can find pork without bone in most delicatessens in Italy. There they would keep the cooked pork for a week, submerged in olive oil, to be eaten cold. I much prefer to eat it hot, just as it comes out of the oven.

SERVES 4

8 tbsp fresh rosemary, finely chopped

4 garlic cloves, very finely chopped

2 tbsp sea salt

1.5kg (3 lb 5 oz) loin of pork, French trimmed, crackling scored in squares

olive oil for basting

Preheat the oven to 200°C/400°F/Gas 6.

Rub the garlic and salt on to the entire surface of the joint. Rub 2 tbsp of the chopped rosemary over the joint as well. Sprinkle generously with olive oil, then with the rest of the rosemary, and roast in the preheated oven for 2 hours, basting from time to time with fresh olive oil. Reduce the heat to 180°C/350°F/Gas 4, and roast for a further 30 minutes. Eat hot, or leave to get cold.

PATATE AL FORNO

BAKED ROSEMARY POTATOES

This recipe reminds me of my mother, who used to make it to accompany a variety of meat and fish dishes. If she was in a hurry, the meat might be cooked together with the potatoes to save time (and washing up).

SERVES 4–6

4 sprigs fresh rosemary

1.5kg (3 lb 5 oz) firm potatoes, peeled and cut into thick slices

2 large onions, sliced

10 wild garlic leaves, chopped, or 2–3 garlic cloves, chopped (optional)

100ml (3½ fl oz) extra virgin olive oil

salt and pepper to taste

Preheat the oven to 200°C/400°F/Gas 6.

Mix the potatoes, onions, garlic (if using) and seasoning to taste in a bowl, then pour over half the olive oil. Coat everything well with the oil. Spread out in a roasting tray, then pour over the rest of the oil and sprinkle with rosemary leaves. Bake in the preheated oven for 30–40 minutes. When the top layer starts to brown, stir well so that the bottom layer can become brown too. Cook for a further 10 minutes and eat immediately.

erbe

FINOCCHIO

WILD FENNEL *Foeniculum vulgare*

This highly aromatic plant, a member of the parsley family (Umbelliferae), grows wild throughout Europe and is especially prolific near the sea. Of the same family is the cultivated bulb, Florence fennel, which is widely used as a vegetable, particularly in Italy (where it is even eaten for dessert!). Wild fennel only has a small, inedible bulb, and is taller, reaching a height of 60–120cm (2–4 ft), and the whole plant smells of anise (a near relation). The first, very tender shoots appear in late spring and look like little fine-leaved, feathery brushes. These shoots can be eaten raw, in salads, in sauces or to garnish (as can the feathery tops of Florence fennel). It is also a marvellous plant to throw on to charcoal embers to flavour barbecued meat and, especially, fish. Use the stalks for this, as they still retain their essential oils when dried.

One of the most important usable parts of the plant is the seed, which should be collected before the end of the summer when fully formed but not yet completely dried out (so still green). When collecting, check carefully to see whether the centre of each little group of still juicy seeds is stuck together, because a red fly likes to deposit her eggs there. Only gather unaffected seeds which will all be clearly distinct from each other. Fennel seeds are widely used in Italian and Provençal cooking to flavour sweet and savoury dishes alike. There is a famous Tuscan pork salami called *la finocchiona*, for instance. In the south of Italy they bake breads, sweet biscuits and savoury biscuits (called *tarallucci*) with fennel seeds, and also use them to flavour savoury dried figs.

Both herb greenery and seeds have long been credited with medicinal properties. Since Roman times, they have been connected with improved eyesight. Their digestive nature is so well known that fennel seeds are used as a flavouring in babies' gripe water, and seeds are included in the *paan* offered to restaurant diners after an Indian meal.

erbe

PASTA CON LE SARDE

PASTA WITH FENNEL AND SARDINES

The main ingredient in this classic Sicilian dish is fennel, which grows in abundance in the hills of that island. The market in Palermo has many stands piled high with fresh fennel, for every Sicilian loves this particular dish. The use of pine kernels and raisins is typical of Sicilian cooking, a reminder of the early culinary Arab influences.

SERVES 4–6

500g (18 oz) fresh fennel herb (you could also use the feathery tops of Florence fennel)

1 small onion, finely chopped

6 tbsp extra virgin olive oil

2 tbsp pine kernels

2 tbsp raisins

3 anchovy fillets in oil, chopped

500g (18 oz) fresh sardines, gutted and filleted

plain flour for coating

2 eggs, beaten

400g (14 oz) thick spaghetti or bucatini

a little cayenne pepper

2 tbsp chopped toasted almonds

salt and pepper to taste

Cook the fennel in slightly salted water until soft, about 3–5 minutes, and then lift out of the water, saving this to cook the pasta in. Roughly chop the fennel and set aside.

Fry the onion in half the oil for a few minutes, then add the pine kernels and raisins and fry for a few more minutes. Add the fennel and anchovies and cook for a little longer, adding 5 tbsp water to moisten the sauce. Meanwhile, coat the sardines in flour and beaten egg, then fry in the remaining oil until golden. Chop half of the sardines coarsely, then add to the sauce, cooking over a very low heat for about 20 minutes. Season to taste.

Meanwhile, preheat the oven to 180°C/350°F/Gas 4.

Bring the fennel water back to the boil, add the pasta and cook until *al dente*. Drain, then mix well with the sauce. Transfer to a pre-warmed ovenproof dish and lay the rest of the sardine fillets on top. Sprinkle with a little salt, cayenne and the toasted almonds. Bake for 10 minutes in the preheated oven and serve immediately.

erbe

FINOCCHIETTI

SWEET FENNEL TARTLETS

Fennel seeds are used both in Mediterranean and Middle Eastern cuisines. This is a typical recipe adapted from some biscuits brought back from Italy as a present by my wife Priscilla. It is fascinating to develop a brand-new and valuable recipe out of just a few humble ingredients. The tartlets are wonderful with coffee or tea.

MAKES 20 TARTLETS

55g (2 oz) fennel seeds

500g (18 oz) plain flour

15g (½ oz) dry baking yeast

100g (3½ oz) icing sugar

125g (4½ oz) unsalted butter, softened

100ml (3½ fl oz) milk

125ml (4 fl oz) extra virgin olive oil

50ml (2 fl oz) Sambuca liqueur

2 egg yolks, beaten

100g (3½ oz) granulated sugar

55g (2 oz) chopped almonds

Put the flour, yeast, icing sugar and butter into a bowl and mix well. Add the milk and olive oil and stir into a smooth dough. Add the Sambuca and fennel seeds and knead well together. Let the dough rest for 30 minutes.

Meanwhile, preheat the oven to 200°C/400°F/Gas 6.

On a floured work surface, roll the dough out to 3mm (⅛ in) thickness, and then cut out from this circles of 10cm (4 in) in diameter. Brush with the egg yolk, sprinkle with the sugar and almonds, and bake in the preheated oven for 8–9 minutes until golden. When cool store in an airtight jar.

erbe

TARALLI CON FINOCCHIO

SAVOURY FENNEL BISCUITS

These little baked rounds of biscuit dough are a speciality in the south of Italy, and can be both savoury and sweet. Here I've given a recipe for a savoury version, which contains fennel seeds, olive oil and pepper. Rather similar in texture to *grissini*, the circular biscuits are irresistible with *antipasto*, but can serve as a snack at any time.

MAKES BETWEEN 25 AND 35 BISCUITS, DEPENDING ON SIZE

1 tbsp fennel seeds

500g (18 oz) plain flour

55g (2 oz) fresh yeast, diluted in a little warm water, or the equivalent of dried yeast

125ml (4 fl oz) olive oil

1 tbsp coarsely ground black pepper

4 tbsp extra virgin olive oil

salt to taste

Put the fennel seeds and flour into a bowl, then stir in the yeast liquid, the 125ml (4 fl oz) olive oil, the pepper, and some salt to taste. Knead to a smooth dough, then leave to rest for a while.

To make the biscuits, take a small portion of the dough at a time, about the size of an apricot. Using your hands, roll each piece into a sausage shape of about 1.5cm (⅝ in) thick and 15cm (6 in) long. Join the two ends together to form a ring, sealing them with your fingers. Leave to rise for 45 minutes on a clean cloth.

Bring to the boil a large pan of slightly salted water, then carefully add the 'rings' one by one to the water, boiling for 2–3 minutes. When they come to the surface, they are ready. Continue this process, removing and adding each 'ring' separately. Let them dry.

Meanwhile, preheat the oven to 200°C/400°F/Gas 6. Brush the dried cooked rings with a little of the extra virgin olive oil and bake them for 20–30 minutes, or until crisp and golden.

erbe

MAGGIORANA/ORIGANO

MARJORAM/OREGANO *Oreganum spp*

There are several types of *Oreganum*, but the three most important in Europe and America are sweet or knotted marjoram (*O. majorana*), pot marjoram (*O. onites*) and wild marjoram or oregano (*O. vulgare*). The generic name comes from the Greek *oros*, 'mountain', and *ganos* , 'joy', because the herbs flourish on and decorate hillsides throughout Europe and Asia. Most are perennial, but habits and flavours differ depending on how far south the plants grow: a marjoram grown in the heat of a Sardinian summer will behave differently and be much more pungent than one in the cooler climate of southern England. But sweet marjoram, as might be expected, is generally acknowledged to be the finest culinary herb. Wild marjoram is stronger in minty flavour, and pot marjoram is less sweet and strong than either, sometimes even bitter. All are bushy and shrubby, with oval green leaves and mauve to pink to white flowers in the summer. All can be found in the wild, particularly in southern Europe, but are now often commercially cultivated, and can be grown in pots at home.

Marjoram is a meat herb mainly, and is often included in a *bouquet garni*. Oregano is used in much the same way, but in Italy adds its unique flavour to pizzas, tomato sauces for pasta (but *not* Bolognese), to vegetable dishes (of aubergine particularly), breads, biscuits and marinated olives. We used to roam around the Aosta Valley and collect bunches of fresh oregano from the hillsides to take home, where it was greatly appreciated by our mother. She would use it fresh, sprinkled on filleted anchovies with garlic, olive oil and breadcrumbs, to be baked. All the marjorams, particularly oregano, can be very successfully dried, and my mother would use it in *pizzaiola* sauce and in bread salads.

erbe

SALSA PIZZAIOLA

TOMATO SAUCE

This versatile sauce originates from the coastal areas of southern Italy, where a similar sauce containing anchovies is called *marinara*. The tomato sauce may be used to accompany chicken, beef or pork, or swordfish or tuna, or to flavour pasta and rice. It may also be used to top pizzas without cheese. I prefer this sauce when made with wild oregano, but marjoram will work just as well.

SERVES 4–6

2 tbsp fresh oregano (or marjoram) leaves, or 1 tbsp dried

2 garlic cloves or 6 wild garlic leaves

6 tbsp extra virgin olive oil

800g (1¾ lb) fresh Italian tomato pulp (buy in cartons, or use fresh tomatoes, skinned)

1 tbsp salted capers, prepared (see page 139)

salt and pepper to taste

Coarsely chop the herb leaves. Finely chop the garlic. Heat the oil in a pan, then gently fry the garlic until golden. Add the tomato and capers and cook gently for 10 minutes. Add the oregano or marjoram, season to taste and cook for a further 5 minutes.

INSALATA DI PANE

BREAD SALAD

This salad, which in some areas of southern Italy is called *panzanella* or *fresella*, used to be made by my mother when she had bread left over that was a little stale. You can buy ready-baked *fresella* from an Italian delicatessen, but you can simply put some leftover bread in the oven to toast until very dry and hard.

SERVES 4

1 tbsp dried oregano

300g (10½ oz) dried bread, preferably brown

4 large, ripe tomatoes, skinned and finely chopped

2 celery sticks, finely diced

1 bunch spring onions, finely chopped

1 garlic clove, very finely chopped

1 yellow pepper, seeded and cut into thin strips

24 pitted black olives

8 tbsp extra virgin olive oil

2 tbsp white wine vinegar

salt and pepper to taste

Soak the bread in water for 1 minute, and then squeeze out the excess water. Crumble into irregular pieces, then put into a bowl with all the remaining ingredients except for the seasoning. Mix well then leave to rest for an hour. Season to taste and serve as a first course.

erbe

RAFANO SELVATICO

HORSERADISH *Armoracia rusticana*

The first time I encountered horseradish was in Vienna, when I was studying there. It was served, freshly grated, as a condiment with pork sausages called *Debreziner*, a speciality originally from Hungary. These were sold on small stalls – a good snack for a student – until late at night, and I urge you to try them when in Vienna.

The horseradish plant is perennial, and native to Asia, but is now naturalised throughout most of Europe, growing on waste, uncultivated ground, along roadsides and on railway cuttings. It is easily identifiable by its long, dark green, glossy leaves, which can be up to 60cm (2 ft) high, and look very similar to dock. Don't worry about collecting it from busy roads, as the pollution will not have affected the root, the only edible part of the plant. You will have to dig quite deep, as the creamy-brown root can be up to 45cm (18 in) long. (If you are digging to get rid of the plants, be careful not to leave the slightest particle of the root behind, as this will grow very readily – why the plant has become such a pest in many gardens.) Take care when cleaning the root after scrubbing. The flesh contains peppery volatile oils which are released when it is peeled, cut or grated, and the vapours will make you weep more copiously than the strongest onion. Do this outside in the open air!

Horseradish is mainly used as a condiment, or a little is added to a milder base to form

a sauce (cream, soured cream, yoghurt, mayonnaise). Its most famous usage in Britain is as a sauce for roast beef, usually grated fresh (or dried) into cream. It is good with smoked fish as well, a common and popular combination in Scandinavia, Germany, the Baltic countries and Russia. It is eaten with some other meats, fresh fish and eggs, and mixed into savoury apple, beetroot and turnip dishes. You can also combine it with caramelised fruit as they do in Italy, for a relish to accompany boiled meat and cheeses.

The name in English means 'coarse' radish, for horseradish is a member of the Cruciferae, along with radish, cress etc. In French it is *raifort*, 'strong root', and in Italian, *rafano selvatico*. It is rarely used in Italian cooking except in the north, in the Veneto, Trentino and Alto Adige, where there are many Austrian Tyrolean influences.

BISTECCA AL RAFANO

STEAK WITH HORSERADISH

This is hardly a recipe, more an idea of a way to use one of the most pungent and sharp flavourings. I love horseradish freshly grated, it doesn't really need to be made into a sauce. This is very simple, but highly effective.

SERVES 4

4 wonderful sirloin steaks, about 2.5cm (1 in) thick

olive oil for brushing

100g (3½ oz) fresh wild horseradish, peeled

salt to taste

Brush the steaks with the olive oil and salt them on both sides. Place them under a very hot grill and cook for 5 minutes on each side. Transfer to a hot plate and grate the fresh horseradish on top. Eat with a green salad and fried potatoes.

MOSTARDA DI RAFANO E LAMPONI

HORSERADISH AND RASPBERRY RELISH

This is a welcome by-product of the raspberry vinegar recipe on page 35. The raspberries, which were only used to flavour the vinegar, are economically re-used in this relish, which can accompany any cold meats. You may buy raspberries especially for this dish, but you will need to add some vinegar, perhaps about 50ml (2 fl oz), or to your taste.

FILLS A 600G (1 LB 5 OZ) JAR

55g (2 oz) fresh wild horseradish, peeled and grated

raspberry leftovers from the *Raspberry Vinegar* on page 35, about 450g (1 lb)

200g (7 oz) caster sugar

½ tsp cayenne pepper

4 grates of nutmeg

salt and pepper to taste

After draining all the liquid from the raspberries, put everything in a pan and bring to the boil. Simmer for about 5 minutes until the sugar has dissolved. Cool down, then spoon into a sterilised jar with a tight lid. It will keep for a few weeks.

MENTA

MINT *Mentha spp*

There are many types of mint, thought to have been spread throughout Europe by the Romans, and some fourteen to fifteen grow wild in Britain alone, among them apple mint, corn mint, water mint, peppermint (see photograph, right), pennyroyal mint, ginger mint and spearmint (see photograph, left). Some are long-time 'natives' taken into cultivation, some are escaped garden cultivars. They thrive in damp places, by ponds, in woodland clearings, and in compost-rich waste ground. The leaf types vary, some oval, some (like apple) downy, and some very small (like pennyroyal), but all smell sweetly minty in various degrees. All are very invasive too, as they grow not by seed, but by their roots; to contain the roots and prevent unwanted spread, plant in large containers, or surround the plants in the earth with stones or slates.

The mints most commonly used in Britain are spearmint and apple mint (peppermint flavours confectionery, chewing gum etc.). Most famously the British use mint in the mint sauce served with lamb, but it also adds its flavour to new potatoes and peas during cooking. It is used in the Middle East to flavour cucumber and yoghurt salads, and as a similar chutney in India, delicious with *tandoori* chicken. In Italy, three types of mint are used – peppermint, *menta,* along with *mentuccia,* a small-leaved mint (*M. romana*), and a related plant *nepitella (Calamintha nepeta),* the latter popular in Tuscany and Umbria. In Tuscany it is unthinkable not to eat *porcini* with *nepitella,* although I think it a very strange combination. Mint leaves are added to salads, to cooked tripe and vegetable dishes (including courgettes and artichokes). My mother used to make a very strong mint liqueur with alcohol and sugar. We children could only taste this very well diluted, but I still remember that wonderful pungency. Mint drinks are popular elsewhere too – think of the mint tea of Morocco and the mint juleps of the southern United States.

Mint is also very good in sweet dishes, worthy of much more thought than just a simple fresh garnish. It makes a wonderful *granita,* and tastes sublime with both chocolate and oranges. It has been used medicinally over the centuries, most noticeably as a digestive – there is some benefit in the after-dinner mint after all!

erbe

ZUPPA DI PISELLI E MENTA

MINT AND PEA SOUP

When my wife lived in France, the French used to call her '*petit pois à la menthe*', 'little mint pea' because of the English tradition of cooking peas with mint. This gave me the idea for this refreshing soup, although I gather it's not particularly novel in Britain.

SERVES 4

1 bunch fresh wild mint, leaves only, washed

2 medium shallots, finely chopped

55g (2 oz) unsalted butter

800g (1¾ lb) fresh podded green peas (or frozen)

500ml (18 fl oz) chicken or vegetable stock

a pinch of freshly grated nutmeg

100ml (3½ fl oz) *crème fraîche*

salt and pepper to taste

Fry the shallot in the butter until soft, about 5 minutes. Add the peas, stock and mint leaves and simmer for 15–20 minutes (10 minutes if frozen). Transfer the ingredients from the pan to a blender, and blend to a smooth liquid. Return to the pan and add the nutmeg, seasoning to taste and *crème fraîche*. Reheat gently, and then serve immediately, accompanied by some toast or *crostini*. Decorate with extra wild mint leaves.

COTOLETTE D'AGNELLO ALLA MENTA

MINT-STUFFED LAMB CUTLETS

In Italy we use a lot of mint in cooking, and as the British tend to use it mainly with lamb, I decided to combine the two, with a different result.

SERVES 4

12 very thick (about 2.5cm/1 in) lamb cutlets, trimmed to the bone, most fat discarded

plain flour for dusting

3 eggs, beaten

dried breadcrumbs for coating

olive oil for frying

salt and pepper to taste

Stuffing

2 tbsp fresh mint, finely chopped

55g (2 oz) Parma ham, finely chopped

40g (1½ oz) Parmesan cheese, freshly grated

Mix the stuffing ingredients together. Make an incision on the side of each cutlet to make a pocket. Fill the pocket with the stuffing, then close by gently pressing the sides together. Dust the cutlets with flour seasoned with salt and pepper to taste, then dip into the beaten egg and then the breadcrumbs. Coat the stuffed cutlets well. Heat the oil and gently fry the cutlets until golden on both sides, about 3–4 minutes on each side. Serve immediately.

erbe

frutti di bosco

FRUIT, BERRIES AND NUTS

THE FONDEST MEMORIES OF MY CHILDHOOD ARE STRONGLY CONNECTED WITH the natural life in the country, where we made use of every possible fruit, berry or nut growing wild. Grown-ups taught my elder brother, sister and I what to pick, and my mother then showed me how to cook it or how to treat it.

As a teenager, together with my schoolfriends, I felt like a ranger in a large territory around my village, in the hills and mountains that we knew like the back of our hands. We may not have known computer games, but we had healthy red cheeks and our bodies were physically fit, able to walk for hours on end. Invariably, before returning home, our stomachs would be full of berries and nuts. (Incidentally, it was not only wild foods that were targeted by us, because on occasion we visited and borrowed from some of the neighbours' fruit and nut trees…) The biggest celebration was when we came back from a successful hunt for chestnuts. These were given to our parents to be cut with a penknife, then roasted over a bonfire in a perforated pan.

I do not think there is a better feeling than returning home after a satisfying hunt, to share your goods with friends and family. It's not just that fresh wild fruit, berries and nuts taste better, it's the pride in having collected something by yourself, using Mother Nature as your endless supplier.

MIRTILLO

BILBERRY *Vaccinium myrtillus*

The bilberry – also known in Britain as whortleberry, whinberry and blaeberry – is of the same genus as the American cranberry and blueberry. Bilberries are smaller and sweeter in flavour than the cultivated blueberries we import (and have started to grow in selected places in Europe), but look similar; they are so dark blue in colour, with a bloom to the smooth skin, that they can look black. The scrubby low plant is native to Europe and northern Asia, and grows on heaths, moorlands and in woods, most often at some height. Pollution has made the berries difficult to find, particularly in my native Italy, but they have a long history all over Europe. The plants flower from April to June, then fruit from July to September, and in many European countries a special day was traditionally set aside for cropping the berries. This was often done with special wooden 'combs', for the berries otherwise have to be laboriously and individually picked by hand. In Ireland, the first Sunday of August was Fraughan Sunday (Old Irish for bilberry), when whole families – and lovers – would go collecting.

Bilberries – or blueberries – are eaten raw with cream, yoghurt or *crème fraîche*, or in mixed fruit salads (known as *sottobosco* in Italy), or in raw or cooked fruit tarts. They would be excellent in an American bilberry muffin. They make a good sauce for lamb, duck and game, jams and preserves (*confettura di mirtilli* in Italy), and in France a liqueur called Myr, which can substitute for Cassis in the drink Kir. They would add much flavour to a traditional English summer pudding, or my version on page 78. And do try the *Winter Rumpot* on page 70.

In the very early days in the UK, bilberries were used as a dye – pickers' hands and children's mouths are always stained blue-black – and the name in English derives from the Danish *bollebar*, dark berry.

CROSTATA DI MIRTILLI

BILBERRY TART

I made this tart years ago, for my wild mushroom book, but actually the best place for it is in this book. It is an extremely good dessert that I don't hesitate to offer here again.

SERVES 6–8   Pastry

250g (9 oz) plain flour

55g (2 oz) caster sugar

a pinch of salt

100g (3½ oz) unsalted butter, cut into small pieces

4 tbsp dry sherry

Filling

700g (1 lb 9 oz) fresh bilberries (or blueberries)

150g (5½ oz) caster sugar

juice of ½ lemon

3 tbsp water

4 gelatine leaves

To make the pastry, sieve together the flour, sugar and salt, then add the butter, and mix together with your fingertips until the mixture forms crumbs. Add the sherry and mix lightly to make a dough. Cover and put aside in a cool place for at least an hour.

Preheat the oven to 180°C/350°F/Gas 4. Roll out the pastry and use to line a tart tin 25cm (10 in) in diameter. Prick the base all over with a fork, and then bake blind for 15–20 minutes, or until the pastry is cooked.

Meanwhile, take about a third of the berries and put them in a pan together with the sugar, lemon juice and water. Bring to the boil and simmer until the juice takes on some colour and becomes slightly syrupy. Remove from the heat, stir in the gelatine and leave to cool a little. When the gelatine has dissolved, and the pastry and syrup are cold, spread half the jellied syrup in a layer over the bottom of the pastry case. Arrange the remaining berries in a decorative way in the pastry case, then glaze with the remaining jellied syrup. Leave the tart to set and cool completely before serving.

frutti di bosco

FRUTTI DI BOSCO INVERNALI

WINTER RUMPOT

I came across this idea when I was living in Germany, where they collect many varieties of summer fruits according to the season, and layer them together with sugar and alcohol for eating in winter. It is called *Rumtopf*. In this recipe, however, I use only the soft fruit featured in this book. You may use either strong dark rum or even vodka of at least 43 per cent alcohol to preserve them, but in Italy we can get a strong pure spirit of at least 95 per cent. The end result is wonderfully sweet and alcoholic fruit – unfortunately only for grown-ups! – which can be eaten with vanilla ice-cream, pancakes or *pannacotta*.

MAKES ABOUT 1.5KG (3 LB 5 OZ)

500g (18 oz) each of bilberries, raspberries, blackberries and wild or cultivated strawberries

2kg (4½ lb) caster sugar

1.5 litres (2¾ pints) strong rum or vodka (see above)

It is imperative that you do not use all the fruit together at one time. Add them as they come into season. You will need a large glass jar or terracotta pot with a lid. Gather the first fruits to appear in the woods or, if you are lazy, buy them. Hull the fruit as appropriate, then wash them briefly. If using bilberries, they must first be pricked with a needle (so that they can absorb more sugar).

Place the first lot of berries in a bowl, sprinkle with a quarter of the sugar, and leave to macerate for 6 hours. Make sure that the maximum amount of sugar has been absorbed by the fruit. Transfer them to a jar, and pour over about a quarter of the alcohol.

Repeat this procedure with each type of berry as they come into season, and then add to the jar, without stirring. Once you have added the last layer of berries, pour over the remaining alcohol and leave for a couple of months before eating. Make sure the fruits are constantly under the level of the alcohol using a weight, something like a plate.

frutti di bosco

LAMPONE

RASPBERRY *Rubus idaeus*

Raspberries, like blackberries, are members of the rose family, and are native to northern Europe and Asia. Perennial, the canes can grow to about 1.8m (6 ft) high, and they favour open woods and heaths, often at quite a high elevation. The canes are virtually thorn free, possibly the reason why this *Rubus* has become the most common in cultivation. Raspberries thrive in a cool climate, and thus do not usually grow in more southerly countries, but in Italy they can be found wild on mountainsides at up to 1,500m (4,500 ft). They were called *idaeus*, according to Pliny, because they grew on the slopes of Mount Ida; the two identifiable Mount Idas are in the very southerly Crete and Asia Minor, and both mountains are said still to be covered in wild raspberries. We used to gather *lamponi* in the Aosta Valley, particularly the Valle di Champoluc. Some 90 per cent of cultivated raspberries in Britain come from Perthshire in Scotland, where the long and not too hot summer days seem to be perfect; wild populations are most plentiful in Scotland as well. Red, white and yellow berries can be found.

Raspberries are best eaten raw. They go well with cream, yoghurt, *crème fraîche* or cream cheese, and can be puréed for sauces to be used in both sweet and savoury dishes and for fools. They are an essential in summer pudding, and make good jam, jelly, vinegar and relishes (see pages 35 and 63). The loganberry, a cross between the raspberry and blackberry, is a better choice for cooking. Raspberries freeze well because they consist of a cluster of conjoined tiny fruits with seeds in them, or drupelets (as opposed to the strawberry, which is one mass of flesh with seeds on the outside), and can bring back the essence of summer when served in the middle of winter.

frutti di bosco

TARTUFI DI CIOCCOLATO CON SALSA DI LAMPONI

CHOCOLATE TRUFFLES WITH RASPBERRY CREAM

The combination of raspberry and chocolate is irresistible. This consists of two recipes in one – chocolate truffles and a raspberry sauce – to be enjoyed together.

SERVES 8

500g (18 oz) bitter *couverture* chocolate (at least 65% cocoa solids), broken into pieces
50ml (2 fl oz) milk
75ml (2½ fl oz) water
25ml (1 fl oz) dark rum
200ml (7 fl oz) double cream
good cocoa powder for dusting
fresh mint leaves to serve (optional)

Raspberry sauce
500g (18 oz) ripe wild raspberries
juice of ½ lemon
300g (10½ oz) caster sugar

For the raspberry sauce, put the raspberries in a pan over a low heat until they start to burst and release their juices. Add the lemon juice and sugar, and leave to cook for a few minutes to melt the sugar. Strain through a sieve, leaving just the pulp and no seeds.

For the chocolate truffles, put the chocolate, milk, water, rum and 85ml (3 fl oz) of the double cream into a *bain-marie*, and heat gently to melt the chocolate. Leave to get cold, then fold in the remaining double cream, which you have whipped. Put in the fridge for 2 hours, by which time the mixture will be semi-solid.

Using a teaspoon, take a piece of the mixture the size of a walnut. Wet your hands with a few drops of rum, to avoid sticking, and form into a ball. Roll in cocoa powder. Do this with the remaining chocolate mixture. You should have 24–30 truffles, a minimum of 3 per person. Chill until ready to serve.

Pour a little of the raspberry sauce on to serving plates, then top with 3 truffles and decorate with mint if liked.

frutti di bosco

CLAFUTIS DI LAMPONI E MORE

RASPBERRY AND BLACKBERRY CLAFOUTIS

It always gives me great pleasure to create impromptu food which is good enough to be written down as a recipe. Fabrice and Valerie are two friends from Paris who were visiting us in the country. We had just picked some ripe and juicy blackberries and raspberries, and so I invented this extremely easy recipe for them.

SERVES 8

200g (7 oz) raspberries

600g (1 lb 5 oz) ripe blackberries (cleaned weight)

8 medium eggs

300g (10½ oz) caster sugar

150g (5½ oz) plain flour

200g (7 oz) unsalted butter, softened

½ tsp baking powder or 1 sachet Lievito Bertolini Vanigliato (an Italian version)

Preheat the oven to 200°C/400°F/Gas 6. After hulling the berries, briefly wash them.

You can either mix the sponge ingredients in a bowl or alternatively a food processor, which would take you half the time. Beat the eggs first, then stir in the sugar, flour and butter. Mix well, then thoroughly beat in the baking powder.

Grease a baking tin of 30 × 25cm (12 × 10 in) and 5cm (2 in) deep with a little extra butter. Pour the mixture into the tin, then add the blackberries, followed by the raspberries. Bake in the preheated oven for 30 minutes, or until the centre of the cake is solid and not runny. You can serve the cake warm or cold, sprinkled with extra sugar.

frutti di bosco

MORA DI ROVO

BLACKBERRY *Rubus fruticosus*

The *Rubus* genus – which includes blackberries and raspberries, and the very much rarer cloudberries and dewberries – belongs to the rose family, and the blackberry plant shares the protective stem prickliness of roses. The genus originated in Asia, but now grows wild and in cultivation all over the world, introduced by settlers to places as far afield as New Zealand and America. Also known as bramble in Britain, the plant can creep or grow as high as a vine; it is a very successful coloniser of uncultivated and waste ground – and gardens, as many frustrated gardeners can attest. It flowers from May to September, and fruits from August to November. Rather as with bilberries, whole families used to go blackberry picking in August and September – I certainly remember we did when I was a child – but there are inhibitions on picking after the end of September. In England and Scotland, it is said that the devil spits or pisses on the berries then, and indeed the berries do tend to be rather hard and less tasty late in the season.

Blackberry picking is characterised by an equal sense of delight and danger, for the plants are so thorny that hands and clothes can be considerably torn. The juices are a potent dye as well, staining pickers' hands and mouths. But the berries, particularly those picked from the wild, are full of flavour, and can be eaten raw, cooked in tarts and an English autumn pudding (as opposed to summer), and made into a traditional apple and blackberry pie or crumble. In Italy we make *mora di rovo* into jams, preserves and sweet sauces – and you should try them in a *granita*, as on the facing page. In England, a blackberry wine used to be popular; in France they make an *eau de vie de mûre*, and occasionally use blackberries to add depth of colour during wine-making. When I was young, when thirsty I would suck the peeled top of a blackberry shoot. It was very satisfying – and once indeed I tried to cook them like asparagus, served with melted butter.

GRANITA DI PANTELLERIA

BLACKBERRY *GRANITA*

During my last holiday in Pantelleria, a small island in the middle of the Mediterranean (between Sicily and Malta), I consumed a mulberry *granita* every day. Made by a local cook, this helped considerably to cool me down in the intense summer heat. Ripe, scented blackberries can be used in the same way, as indeed can strawberries, raspberries or other soft fruit.

MAKES ABOUT 3KG (6½ LB)

1.5kg (3 lb 5 oz) very ripe blackberries, cleaned

juice of 2 lemons

finely grated zest of 1 lemon

1.5kg (3 lb 5 oz) caster sugar

4–6 fresh mint leaves

Put the berries in a stainless-steel pot over a medium heat and let them burst and release their juices, stirring from time to time. Add the lemon juice and zest, followed by the sugar, and cook for 15 minutes, still stirring. When the sugar has melted, leave the mixture to cool. The berries will have almost dissolved, so there should be no need to strain, but if you are sensitive to texture, you can do so.

To make the *granita,* take 2–3 tbsp mixture per person and dilute with half its volume of water. Mix well and then place in a suitable container in the freezer. When the mixture starts to set, remove from the freezer and stir well to break up the ice crystals. Return to the freezer. Repeat this process a couple of times, or until the crystals have been completely dispersed and the *granita* is evenly grainy. Spoon into glasses, decorate with a mint leaf on top, and serve immediately.

frutti di bosco

MERINGA ESTIVA

ITALIAN SUMMER PUDDING

This Italian 'summer pudding' has to be my favourite dessert because it combines the essence of summer, embodied in a variety of berries, with the meringue, which gives a nice dry and sweet texture. I serve it regularly in my restaurant, but have to resort occasionally to using cultivated berries, although I can assure you that wild ones taste much better.

Ideally the meringue should be piped into the shape of a cornucopia, a tapering 'container' for the berries, but it's probably easier to make rounds with a depression in the centre.

SERVES 4

Meringue

5 large egg whites

a pinch of salt

300g (10½ oz) caster sugar (half could be replaced by vanilla sugar)

Sauce

225g mixed berries (ripe, even over-ripe, are best)

about 6 tsp water

85g (3 oz) caster sugar

Filling

115g (4 oz) each of blueberries, raspberries and blackberries

55g (2 oz) each of wild strawberries and redcurrants

55g (2 oz) caster sugar

juice of 1 lime

To start the meringues, preheat the oven to 110°C/225°F/Gas ¼, and line a baking sheet with greaseproof paper. Whisk the egg whites in a clean bowl with the salt and 2 tbsp of the sugar. Gradually add more sugar as you continue whisking, until you have used up all the sugar and the mixture is stiff and glossy. Put the meringue carefully into a piping bag. Pipe cornucopia-shaped meringues on to the baking sheet; you should get about 10–12. Bake dry in the very low oven for 4–5 hours until perfectly crisp and white. Allow the meringues to cool, then keep in an airtight container until needed.

To make the sauce, place the berries in a saucepan with the water. Place over a low heat and allow all the berries to burst and release their juices, a few minutes only. Strain the berries and their juices through muslin into another pan. Do not force through, just allow to drip. Discard the berries, and add the sugar to the liquid. Heat gently until you have a syrupy sauce. Leave to become cold.

When ready to serve, put all the cleaned fruit for the filling into a bowl, and add the sugar and lime juice. Gently toss without damaging the berries. Put a meringue on each plate and divide the berries between them, filling the cornucopia shape and also allowing some to spill over on to the plate. Spoon some sauce on to each plate, and serve immediately.

frutti di bosco

FIORI E BACCHE DI SAMBUCO

ELDER (FLOWER AND BERRY) *Sambucus nigra*

The elder tree is native to Europe, western Asia and North America.
In folklore tradition, it is a tree of powerful magic: the Cross was reputedly made of elderwood; if the wood is burned, you will see the devil; but if the tree is planted outside your house, you will keep the devil at bay. The elder can bring bad luck but, more practically, the leaves keep flies away. The trees, which grow in hedgerows, woods, on chalk downs and in compost-rich waste ground, are considered to be a pest by many. They can reach a height of about 10m (30 ft), but are often more shrub-like. The centre wood is hard, while the side branches are often hollow, used by children to make peashooters, arrows and pens. Another use is as a 'nursery' for a type of edible gelatinous fungus called Judas ear; the fungi grow on the trunk and branches of elders, particularly older specimens (see page 128). The tree grows very rapidly, and was once cultivated as hedging.

The principal use of the elder nowadays is as food. Its white flowers, which bloom in June and July, have a sweet, to some a slightly sickly, odour and flavour, thought to resemble that of the muscat grape. All over Europe, bunches of the flowers are added to jams, wines, jellies and stewed fruits (particularly gooseberries) to contribute their unique flavour. Flower heads are also dipped in batter and deep-fried as fritters. An elderflower 'champagne', made in England for many years, was forced to change its name in 1994 by French growers in Champagne. The small, black berries, which appear in September and October, are made into a cordial or elixir (mine is particularly good for coughs and colds) and a wine, and are often used to deepen flavour and colour in lesser wines and ports. They are good in jams, jellies, relishes and vinegars, and are often included in a mixed fruit soup in Scandinavia.

frutti di bosco

ELISIR DI FRUTTI DI SAMBUCO

ELDERBERRY ELIXIR

This elixir has more than once alleviated my winter cold symptoms!
Add it to sparkling wine, or pour over ice-cream.

MAKES 1.5 LITRES (2¾ PINTS)

2kg (4½ lb) elderberries, cleaned

100ml (3½ fl oz) water

10 cardamom seeds

15 cloves

2 cinnamon sticks

juice and rind of 1 lemon

1kg (2¼ lb) caster sugar

500ml (18 fl oz) Scotch whisky, brandy or even a
    dark rum (optional)

Cook the berries with the water for 20 minutes, or until all the berries have burst. Squash against the side of the pan, to squeeze out the maximum juice. When cool, put into a cloth over a bowl to strain, as you would when making jelly. Squeeze all the remaining juice through the cloth into the bowl and discard the pulp. You should have about 1 litre (1¾ pints) juice. Put this into a saucepan with the spices, lemon juice and rind. Cook for 10 minutes, then add the sugar and heat to melt. When melted, bring back to the boil and cook for a further 10 minutes.

Let this liquid cool a little, then strain. Decant the elixir into sterilised bottles, where it will keep for a long time. Add the alcohol if you like: the end result will make a nice *digestif*.

FRITTATA DI FIORE DI SAMBUCO

ELDERFLOWER FRITTATA

This recipe is like a cross between a fritter and an omelette.

SERVES 4

6 tbsp elderflowers

2 tbsp olive oil

8 medium eggs

finely grated zest of 1 lemon

2 tbsp plain flour

55g (2 oz) caster sugar

a pinch of salt

1 lemon, quartered

Remove all the stems from the tiny white flowers. Pour the olive oil into a 20cm (8 in) non-stick frying pan, add the elderflowers and heat gently. Beat the eggs well, then add the lemon zest, flour, half the sugar and the salt. Pour the mixture into the pan and fry until the underside forms a crust and the top is almost solid. Serve hot or cold with lemon quarters and the rest of the sugar sprinkled over the top. Cut into wedges to serve.

FRAGOLINE DI BOSCO

WILD STRAWBERRY *Fragaria vesca*

The tiny wild strawberry was the only strawberry known to Europe
until the discovery of the New World. Until then, any cultivation was of strawberry runners taken from the wild into gardens, and the size of the fruit could not be improved. Not until the native fruit was hybridised with larger and juicier wild fruits brought back from South and North America in the seventeenth and eighteenth centuries, did strawberries manage to achieve anything like the form and size they are today.

Wild strawberries are still a delight though, if rare, and their taste is more intensely fragrant than that of the garden strawberry. They grow in open woodland and scrub, and can be used as attractive ground cover in flowerbeds in the garden. They were all over the mountains near Avellino, where we would gather basketfuls in season – always leaving some for the birds! They flower from April to July, and fruit from late June to August. The English name has nothing to do with straw, but derives from the Anglo-Saxon '*streow*', to strew, referring to the way in which the plants propagate, by sending shoots or runners straying out in all directions.

Wild strawberries, because they are such a rare – and expensive – treat, need nothing else done to them, perhaps a little sugar, lemon juice or balsamic vinegar in the Italian tradition, or a little red wine. The French macerate them with orange juice and an orange liqueur. If you have a glut, you could use them as you would garden strawberries, in fruit salads, open tarts, fools and purées. They would also be good in a *Rumpot* (see page 70).

FRAGOLINE DI BOSCO AL BALSAMICO

WILD STRAWBERRIES WITH BALSAMIC VINEGAR

To make this unusual recipe, apart from fresh wild strawberries, you will need a speciality from Modena in Emilia Romagna. This is balsamic vinegar, which is the cooked-down juice of the Trebbiano grape. This becomes vinegar when it is aged in special wooden barrels for at least fifteen to twenty years (and up to fifty!). It is called 'balsamic' due to the fact that it was used as a balm or medicine to relieve cold symptoms. Today balsamic vinegar has become very fashionable, but it is not for this reason that I combine it with the strawberries. It simply enhances their flavour so well.

SERVES 4

500g (18 oz) wild strawberries, cleaned

150g (5½ oz) caster sugar

4 tbsp aged balsamic vinegar (or *Raspberry Vinegar*, see page 35)

4–8 mint leaves

Put the strawberries into a bowl with the sugar and leave to macerate for an hour. Just before serving, mix with the vinegar and decorate with mint leaves.

MARMELLATA DI FRAGOLINE DI BOSCO

WILD STRAWBERRY JAM

When you have a glut of wild strawberries, transform them into a jam so that you can enjoy their wonderful flavour throughout the winter.

MAKES ABOUT 1KG (2¼ LB)

600g (1 lb 5 oz) ripe wild strawberries, cleaned

500g (18 oz) caster sugar

pared rind and juice of 1 lemon

Put the cleaned strawberries into a pan, then add 50ml (2 fl oz) water. Bring to the boil, and simmer until the strawberries are soft. Add the sugar and lemon rind and juice and cook until the sugar has melted. Simmer for about 10 minutes, then test for setting. Put a little on a cold saucer (keep a couple of saucers in the freezer). If it wrinkles when you push your finger through it, setting point has been reached. If still a little liquid, simmer for a few more minutes, then test again.

When ready, cool the jam a little then remove the lemon rind. Pour the jam into sterilised jars, leave to cool completely, and then seal with a tight lid.

frutti di bosco

CASTAGNA/MARRONE

SWEET CHESTNUT *Castanea sativa*

Sweet chestnut trees are native to western Asia, and were introduced to Europe by the Ancient Greeks. They flourish in southern Europe, and there are large forests in the Apennines and Pre-Alps in Italy, in the Ardèche in France, and in Spain and Portugal. The Romans brought them to Britain, where they have naturalised, but the fruit is never so successful as it is in the warmer south. (Some British trees, though, are extremely long-lived and have enormously wide trunks.) Sweet chestnuts are not related to horse chestnuts – 'conker' trees – but have similar fruits, the nuts or kernels held within a prickly outer casing or burr. In Italy, *castagne* or wild chestnuts, have two or three small nuts within one burr; *marroni*, the fruit of grafted, cultivated trees, have one nut per burr only.

Chestnuts are used much more widely on the Continent than in Britain, and at one time were considered a staple food, because they are so high in carbohydrate. They are particularly important in the diet of those living in the Italian mountains and hills, where they are dried and kept all year round. They are cooked in milk for breakfast, and used as a vegetable. They are ground to a flour and used in flatbreads and biscuits, and to make pasta and polenta (the latter commonplace before maize was introduced from the New World). Chestnut flour is used as a thickener, and to make a wonderful cake, *castagnaccio* (see page 86). The purée is used in the famous *monte bianco*, a mound of sweetened chestnut ice-capped with whipped cream. The larger and sweet *marroni* make the luxury *marroni canditi*, or *marrons glacés*. Dried chestnuts soaked in water and cooked are served with Alpine butter as an *antipasto*.

Dried chestnuts are available, and they should be soaked in water according to the instructions on the packet. Frozen chestnuts have recently come on to the market as well.

The fondest memory I have of chestnuts comes from childhood. My mother would get up quite early to boil some. These were still hot when we left to go to school, secreted in our trouser pockets to warm our hands.

MARRONI CANDITI

CANDIED CHESTNUTS

Make a small slit in the shell of each chestnut and blanch in boiling water for about 5 minutes. The shells will then detach easily. During the cooking and candying process, it is quite normal that a few of the chestnuts will break into pieces. This doesn't matter at all, because the pieces will taste just as good as the whole nuts.

MAKES ABOUT 1KG (2¼ LB)

800g (1¾ lb) chestnuts, shelled weight	750g (1 lb 10 oz) caster sugar
1 tsp salt	3 vanilla pods
3 bay leaves	100g (3½ oz) icing sugar (optional)

After peeling off the dark brown skin from the chestnuts, leave the second paler brown skin intact. Put the chestnuts into a large casserole and cover with water. Bring to the boil, then add the salt and bay leaves. Cook very gently for 30 minutes. Replace the water, which will now be brown, with more boiling water and boil for a further 30 minutes, keeping the bay leaves in. Cool the chestnuts down slightly by adding some cold water to the pan, and set aside.

Meanwhile, put the caster sugar into a pan with 500ml (18 fl oz) water, and let the sugar melt over a gentle heat until clear. Cut the vanilla pods lengthways, scrape out the sticky black seeds and add these and the pods to the hot syrup.

Now drain the chestnuts and, while still warm and using a sharp knife, remove the second skin very carefully. Try not to break the nuts. Lay them in a tray and then pour over the hot syrup. Leave to rest at room temperature for 24 hours.

The next day collect the syrup, heat it up and then pour it over the chestnuts again. Repeat this process for another two to three days, or until the colour of the nuts has changed to a darker brown, and the syrup has penetrated to the centre of the nuts.

You now have the option of keeping the chestnuts in a jar with the syrup, or making them into real *marrons glacés*, which are dry, with a sugar crust.

To make *marrons glacés*, the chestnuts must first be drained of the syrup, then placed on a rack over a tray. Prepare a liquid glaze by diluting the optional icing sugar in a little water. Pour this over the chestnuts, each time re-collecting the liquid and pouring over again until a decent glaze has been obtained. Leave the nuts to dry and then keep in an airtight container. Home-produced candied chestnuts never keep for very long.

frutti di bosco

MARRONI AL GRAND MARNIER

CHESTNUTS WITH GRAND MARNIER

If using fresh chestnuts, cook them as in the previous recipe, and candy them. You could always buy a jar of chestnuts in syrup, or *marrons glacés*.

SERVES 4

12 chestnuts in syrup or *Candied Chestnuts* (see previous recipe)

55g (2 oz) icing sugar

300ml (10 fl oz) double cream, whipped

2 tbsp Grand Marnier

12 fresh bay leaves, in perfect condition

Drain the chestnuts from their syrup. Mix the sugar with the whipped cream and then fold in the liqueur. Make 3 *quenelles* from the mixture, using 2 dessertspoons. Place the *quenelles* on a dessert plate, and position a chestnut on top of each one. Do the same on 3 other plates. Pour over a little of the chestnut syrup, and decorate with the bay leaves before serving.

CASTAGNACCIO

CHESTNUT CAKE

In Tuscany and northern Italy in winter, street vendors used to sell irregular pieces of warm chestnut cake from a large tray, but now *castagnata* is available in traditional *pasticcerie* and in bars.

Ensure that you only use the most recent season's chestnut flour – produced in the autumn – as it doesn't keep for very long.

SERVES 10

700g (1 lb 9 oz) chestnut flour

a pinch of salt

85g (3 oz) caster sugar

5 tbsp extra virgin olive oil

2 tbsp pine kernels

1 tsp fennel seeds

200g (7 oz) seedless raisins

1 sprig fresh rosemary, leaves only

Preheat the oven to 180°C/350°F/Gas 4.

Put the flour, salt and 55g (2 oz) of the sugar into a bowl, then add 2 tbsp of the oil and enough water to obtain a fairly soft, almost runny mixture. Use a little of the oil to grease a 25cm (10 in) baking tray, and pour the mixture into it, levelling the top with a spatula. Scatter the pine kernels, fennel seeds, raisins and rosemary needles over the entire surface. Pour over the rest of the oil and sprinkle with the remaining sugar. Bake for 40–45 minutes in the preheated oven. Serve warm, in slices, but it can also be eaten cold.

MELA SELVATICA

CRAB APPLE *Malus sylvestris*

The small wild crab apple, *Malus sylvestris,* is native to Europe, and a near relative, *M. pumila var. mitis* grows in the Caucasus. The latter is slightly larger than the former, and both played important roles in the development of the modern apple as we know it. Crab apple trees are still used today as cultivated apple rootstock. However, unlike some fruits which only achieved recognisable modern form quite recently, the apple has been in cultivation for at least 3,000 years. The Romans are said to have known at least twenty varieties.

Crab apple trees can be found in woods, hedges and scrub, and are common in Britain and northern Europe, although rarer here than apple trees which have developed from dropped cultivated apple pips (known as 'wildings'). As with all apples, a cooler climate is required, for apples need a cold period in winter, and I do not remember crab apples – known in Italian as *meline selvatiche* – from my childhood. It was in Britain that I first made their acquaintance. The trees flower in May and fruit from August to November, best in September and October. The ripe yellow, green or red fruit is a small apple shape and is extremely astringent (giving rise in English to 'sour' words like 'crabby'), and one of its earliest appearances in English cooking was in the sour sauce, verjuice, used in cooking in the Middle Ages as we might use lemon juice. Crab apples make a wonderful pectin-rich jelly, a jam, a fruit cheese, can be roasted whole as an accompaniment to meat, and have been made into a wine. I have also candied them with horseradish to use as a pickle.

frutti di bosco

MELINE AL RAFANO

CRAB APPLE AND HORSERADISH RELISH

This idea came to me when eating *mostarda di Cremona*, the caramelised mixed fruit jam-preserve from Italy, which is used to accompany boiled meats, game (see page 202) and cheese. In this recipe I use freshly grated wild horseradish, which is very strong, but you can also make it with ready-grated horseradish from a jar. If you like, you can experiment with other fruit: I would suggest quinces, pears, apricots or pomegranates.

MAKES ABOUT 3KG (6½ LB)

2kg (4½ lb) small crab apples, with stems

1.5kg (3 lb 5 oz) preserving sugar

500ml (18 fl oz) water

200g (7 oz) freshly peeled and grated wild horseradish

Wash the crab apples, then pat dry. Put the sugar and water into a pan over a low heat. Let the sugar melt until it is transparent, then add the crab apples. Bring back to a gentle simmer, and leave to cook for an hour on a very low heat. Let it rest for one to two days at room temperature in order to absorb more of the sugar.

Bring back to simmering point, then add the grated horseradish. Cook and stir for a further 30 minutes. Leave to cool, then bottle. It will keep for a long time.

frutti di bosco

GELATINA DI MELINE

CRAB APPLE JELLY

I am always reluctant to use well-known preserving recipes, but this one is so good – so much pleasure from so little work! I like to eat it as a jam for breakfast, or as an accompaniment for roasts.

MAKES 1–1.5KG (2¼–3 LB 5 OZ) JELLY, DEPENDING ON THE APPLES

2kg (4½ lb) crab apples, washed and halved

caster sugar as required (see below)

rind of 1 lemon

Cover the fruit with water in a large pan, and boil until soft and pulped.

You now need to use a jelly bag (or piece of muslin) to obtain the juice. I always tie the strings of the bag to the four legs of an upside-down chair or stool with a bowl below to catch the pure juice. This could take a few hours, or overnight.

Once you have collected all the juice, weigh it and then weigh out the same amount of sugar. Bring the juice to the boil, and add the measured sugar and the lemon rind. Cook gently to melt the sugar, then bring back to the boil for 1 minute before testing for a set. Do so by putting a small amount on a cold saucer (keep a couple of saucers in the freezer). If it wrinkles when pushed with a finger, it is ready; if it is still a little liquid, simmer for a few minutes more.

Cool the jelly a little, then transfer to a sterilised jar, discarding the lemon rind. Leave to cool completely and then seal tightly.

frutti di bosco

NOCCIOLA

HAZELNUT *Corylus avellana*

The hazelnut is a low shrubby tree found in woods, scrub and hedges, but it can grow to about 6m (20 ft) tall. It is native to Turkey, but now flourishes throughout Europe and elsewhere (there are related species in Asia and North America), especially in Italy, in Campania, Lazio, Piedmont and Sicily. The city of Avellino in Campania probably takes its name from the product for which it is most celebrated. One hazel variety, 'Tonda Gentile delle Langhe', grows in the same area as the white truffle, and truffles grown beside hazel trees are said to be the best! The trees flower from December to April, and the familiar nuts, encased in a hard shell, appear from late August to October. The English name derives from the Anglo-Saxon *haesil*, a cap, hat or headdress. Cob and filbert are two English names for cultivated hazelnuts.

Hazelnuts have been used as food for thousands of years. The nuts are milky and juicy when fresh in the autumn, but their sweetness develops as the nuts mature and dry. Like any other nut, though, the oils can turn rancid if too old or badly stored. The nuts are very nutritious, containing a good balance of oil, protein, vitamins and minerals. In most countries which use hazels, they are made into biscuits, cakes and confectionery – notably, in Italy, nougat and *gianduiotto* chocolates (little triangles with a high proportion of hazelnut paste). Not to forget the well-known *nutella*, a chocolate and hazelnut spread, which takes me back to my childhood in Italy… Hazelnut oil is delicate and delicious, and there is even an Italian hazelnut liqueur (marketed in a bottle shaped like a monk!).

Hazel trees are coppiced, and the pliable canes are used in water divining and were once a principal source of the wattle for wattle and daub walls. Hazel branches, because they are so long and straight, are the best for carving into walking sticks (see page 8).

NOCCIOLE AL MIELE

ROASTED WILD HAZELNUTS IN HONEY

If every year were as good as the year 2000 for collecting hazelnuts, then you would have no difficulty collecting enough to make this recipe. In fact most years, in competition with the squirrels, I collect quite a few from around my country home. This simple recipe is very rewarding when you are not too busy, and as for eating the nuts, once you start it will be difficult to stop! You can make this recipe with other nuts such as almonds, walnuts or cashews.

FILLS A 600G (1 LB 5 OZ) JAR

300g (10½ oz) shelled wild hazelnuts

300g (10½ oz) acacia honey

Roast the hazelnuts (see page 93), about 5–10 minutes – watch them *very* carefully or they will burn – then rub off the skins. Leave to cool.

Put the nuts in an airtight jar, and then pour over the honey. I have to admit I eat the nuts out of the jar with a spoon …

frutti di bosco

CROCCANTE DI NOCCIOLE

WILD HAZELNUT CRUNCH

Almost every year I make these sweets a couple of weeks before Christmas and store them in an airtight jar to keep them crisp. I then put them into little individual cellophane bags to give as presents. A little care is needed when cooking them, as the liquid caramelised sugar used to make the hazelnuts stick together is extremely hot and can burn: I use a half lemon as my shaping tool to save my fingers.

You will also need about ten sheets of rice paper.

MAKES 1KG (2¼ LB)

700g (1 lb 9 oz) hazelnuts, shelled weight

thinly pared rind of ½ lemon and ½ orange

700g (1 lb 9 oz) caster sugar

6 tbsp good-quality runny honey

½ lemon

Preheat the oven to 230°C/450°F/Gas 8.

Put the shelled hazelnuts in a metal tray and roast in the preheated oven for about 5–10 minutes until the skins crack, but the hazelnuts remain pale brown in colour. Watch them very carefully, as they can burn easily. When they have cooled a little, rub the nuts together in a cloth (or shake in a sieve), and the skins should come off easily. Leave to become completely cold.

Slice the lemon and orange rind into fine strips, and then into cubes. Put the sugar in a heavy-bottomed pan along with the honey over a medium to strong heat. Stirring most of the time, cook until the sugar and honey have become liquid and turn brown in colour: this takes about 10 minutes. At this point add the rind and nuts to the caramel in the pan. Stir, keeping the pan on the heat until all the nuts are well coated. Remove from the heat.

Now lay out the sheets of rice paper and make large heaps of the hazelnut caramel. The nuts tend to stick up from the caramel: wait until you reach the bottom of the pan and use the remaining caramel to fill up any gaps around the nuts. Flatten the heaps by patting down with the lemon half – but take care, as they will still be very hot. Leave to cool a bit, but when still warm, cut with a large knife into 2 × 3cm (¾ × 1¼ in) pieces. Store in airtight jars.

frutti di bosco

NOCE

WALNUT *Juglans regia*

The walnut tree is native to temperate regions stretching from southern Europe across Asia to China, and has been introduced to the Americas, Australasia and southern Africa. There is extensive cultivation in California, China, France and Italy.

The fruit of the walnut tree is what is known as a green drupe: a fleshy husk surrounds a hard-shelled stone or nut, within which is the edible, brain-like kernel. When still unripe, usually about late June, the whole fruit can be used – fleshy husk, still soft nut shell, kernel and all – to make the famous *nocino* liqueur. These green walnuts are also the ones that are pickled in Britain. I can well remember how we children used to think we 'owned' all the walnut trees. We would throw wooden sticks up and a rain of green walnuts would fall on to our heads. For days afterwards our hands would be stained brown from the strong dye in the green skins. At a later stage, the husk becomes thinner and tougher, and the shell hardens around the kernel. These fresh half-ripe kernels are removed from the shells, skinned then macerated in syrup, a Middle Eastern speciality. Or the fruit are allowed to become fully mature, usually in November, when they are washed and dried in the sun.

Much of the British crop of walnuts is plucked green for pickling, but in other countries the mature fruits are a very important culinary crop. The significance of the walnut in both France and Italy is perhaps indicated by the name – *noix* and *noce* respectively – both of which mean 'nut' in general as well as 'walnut'. The nut kernels are eaten in the hand – popular all over Europe at Christmas time – or used in salads and cereal dishes. The kernels are ground to be baked in cakes and biscuits, and used in ice-creams and confectionery. A number of savoury walnut sauces exist. In Italy, walnuts are often added to the pine kernels in a pesto, and minced walnuts are used with olive oil, garlic and Parmesan for a sauce to dress a Ligurian speciality called *pansôti al preboggion*.

Very ripe kernels are pressed to make walnut oil in France.

NOCI AL CIOCCOLATO

WALNUTS IN CHOCOLATE

On grand occasions such as Christmas, when the meal goes on for hours, these would be delightful served after coffee perhaps, with a glass of Moscato wine.

To make this recipe work, there are two important elements. One is good chocolate *couverture* with at least 65–70 per cent cocoa solids. The other is a sugar thermometer to measure the temperature of the melted chocolate. In fact, the hardening of the melted chocolate around the walnuts is only possible if you are using the following method.

MAKES 36 CHOCOLATE NUTS

36 shelled walnut halves, from the newest crop

125g (4½ oz) chocolate *couverture* with at least 65–70% cocoa solids

Melt the chocolate in a double boiler – it must never be over direct heat – and warm up to the temperature of 45–50°C/122°F. Once melted, remove from the heat.

Immerse the individual walnut halves in the melted chocolate one by one, making sure they are completely coated. Place them on a rack over a tray to allow for dripping, or on greaseproof paper. Once cool, detach from the rack or paper and store in an airtight jar.

frutti di bosco

SALAME DI FICHI, DATTERI E NOCI

FIG, DATE AND WALNUT SALAMI

In the southern areas of Italy it is quite common to use dry fruit to make something very special. This recipe requires no cooking, as I use walnuts, dried figs and dates. The result is a sausage-shaped 'salami' which can be enjoyed in slices with coffee or a good dessert wine. It also accompanies cheese very well.

You could make a slightly different version to that offered here. Replace the orange peel with 125g (4½ oz) pine kernels and add 1 tbsp fennel seeds. Omit the vanilla and pepper. Franco Taruschio, my friend from Wales, makes his own version of this, which reflects the region he comes from, the Marche.

You will need some rice paper, foil and greaseproof paper.

MAKES ABOUT 1.5KG (3 LB 5 OZ)

200g (7 oz) shelled walnuts

500g (18 oz) dried figs, hard stems removed

500g (18 oz) dried dates, pitted (Medjool are the best)

150g (5½ oz) candied lemon peel (cedro lemon), diced

125g (4½ oz) candied orange peel, diced

1 tbsp ground black pepper

1 vanilla pod, split, or a few drops of vanilla essence

Halve the walnuts. Chop the figs into small pieces, then blend them in a food processor until a sticky paste is obtained. Repeat with the dates, then transfer the figs and dates to a bowl. Add the walnut halves, orange and lemon peel, pepper and vanilla seeds (scrape out from the pod). Mix together well, to a sticky paste studded with walnuts.

Transfer half of this paste on to some foil, and then carefully shape into a large sausage about 30cm (12 in) in length and 6cm (2½ in) thick. Lay a sheet of rice paper out on the work surface, and then transfer the sausage out of the foil on to it, rolling it up tightly as the paper sticks to the mixture. Then envelop the sausage in a sheet of greaseproof paper, rolling up tightly once again. Tie up with string, then store in a cool, dry place for about a month before eating. Do the same with the remaining mixture, to make a second sausage.

Unwrap from the greaseproof paper, and cut into slices before eating.

frutti di bosco

funghi

FUNGI

WHEN I FIRST CAME TO ENGLAND IN 1975, I SOON DISCOVERED THAT I WAS IN A mushroom paradise, but one where few people were interested in collecting and eating. All the more for me!

Mushrooms and other fungi are unique in that, unlike all other plants, they do not convert the sun's rays into energy. What they do is obtain nutrition from animal and vegetable matter, living or dead. In fact, without mushrooms and the rest of the fungi world, we could not exist. They are solely responsible for the breaking down of dead matter, thereby transforming it into valuable nourishment for the continuation of life. Many fungi are parasitic, attacking living plants, especially trees, in time reducing them to dust. And other forms of fungi exist, without which our stock of basic foods would be very much diminished. The fungus which is yeast is used in bread and wine making, a mould fungus is important in many blue cheeses, for instance, and moulds are also used in the fermentation of many foods vital in the East, notably soy beans.

Fungi are composed of minute filaments that cannot be seen by the naked eye. These hair-like filaments – or hyphae – combine to form a cobweb-like mat called the mycelium, and it is this mycelium which grows through the material upon which the fungus feeds. When two mycelia meet, and conditions are right, a new fruiting body, a mushroom, is formed. Mushrooms are self-seeding, with gills containing spores (seeds) which are only visible under a microscope. Most mushrooms are 'spore-droppers', their spores dropping naturally from the gills, or being swept off and away by wind and rain. Other mushrooms, which include the morel, the truffles and cup fungi, are ascomycetes or 'spore-shooters'. Their spores are formed in sacs on the surface of the plants, and when the mushrooms are mature, the spores are shot out.

Man's fascination with mushrooms has been in existence since the beginning of time. Some mushrooms are poisonous, some are hallucinogenic, and some contain medicinal properties – the Chinese, for instance, have used curative fungus extracts for many thousands of years. In the West, the most important medicinal discovery was that of the fungus which was developed into the life-saving penicillin.

However, it is the fruiting body of the mushroom that is of primary interest to most gourmets the world over. The taste and appearance of the flesh are the most important elements, and they always represent a culinary treat, either by themselves or in combination with game or fish. They are also rather good for you, as they contain a virtually fat-free protein, with all the essential amino acids, and a variety of other valuable nutrients.

In order to collect wild mushrooms, a good knowledge of the subject is required, otherwise it could turn out to be your last supper. I can never stress enough how important it is not to pick and eat anything, however good it looks or smells, unless you are completely and utterly sure of its edibility.

The individual characteristics of each mushroom are described in their introductions, but there are some general rules which should be followed when mushroom picking.

1 Hunt with an expert (the Mycological Society provides tuition).

2 Go equipped with a basket, knife, walking stick and sturdy boots/clothing, according to the weather.

3 Avoid mushroom picking in the rain, as mushrooms absorb a great deal of water.

4 Clean the mushrooms immediately to avoid contaminating the rest in the basket.

5 Never use a plastic bag to carry mushrooms, as the proteins degenerate quite quickly when enclosed in warm conditions without air to breathe.

6 Never collect or destroy poisonous mushrooms, as they are important in the natural cycle.

7 If a mushroom has been nibbled by snails, do not assume that it will be safe for human consumption. *Amanita phalloides*, or death cap, is the most poisonous of all mushrooms, and is regularly eaten by snails without them suffering any ill effects.

8 Try not to go picking alone in deep forests, and if you do, remember the route back!

9 Take some drinking water and a sandwich if you plan a long walk.

10 If you like, take a mobile phone for security – I never do, though, and I would hate to do so!

11 Collect only the mushrooms you need for yourself, leaving some for other pickers (this is very difficult to do).

12 Do not trespass on private property.

13 Leave the environment as you found it, taking your rubbish with you.

14 If you want to pick the best, you will have to go early in the morning – this avoids most other competition as well.

15 When you find a rich picking ground, remember it, and note the date, as it may be possible to find mushrooms there next year as well. Don't tell anyone else, though!

16 It is possible to cut the mushrooms from their base with a knife, but most mushrooms can be pulled from the earth. The efficient spore distribution will ensure that more will grow in the same place.

17 Do not trust the old wives' tales which aver that inedibility is certain if parsley turns yellow, garlic green and silver black during cooking, because there are some poisonous mushrooms that will not cause this reaction.

18 Do not let all these restrictions deter you, as they are necessary to ensure the survival of mushrooms in the future. Mushrooms were among the first forms of vegetation on the planet, and we should protect them.

Happy hunting!

PORCINO

CEP OR PENNY BUN *Boletus edulis*

There are many varieties of *Boletus,* but *B. edulis* or cep is to my mind the best – my beloved *porcino*. In fact I think it is probably the ultimate wild mushroom. Usually 8–20cm (3¼–8 in) in diameter, sometimes 30cm (12 in), its cap is hemispherical at first, becoming flatter as it matures. Its colour varies from pale to dark brown, and the 'glossy' look explains its Victorian alternative name of 'penny bun' – it actually looks like a well baked and glazed round bun. The stem is white with a surface network of veins, appearing to be part of the cap at first, but becoming longer and bulbous at the base as the cap matures and separates from it. *B. edulis* can be found in grass in or near mixed woodland, usually singly, but sometimes in groups of two or three, from early summer to the first frosts of late autumn. It usually grows near oak, birch, beech and pine, but also on sandy soil.

The cep is probably the most important of the wild mushrooms, particularly in my native Italy, where it is eaten fresh with relish, but also preserved by drying – the famous *funghi porcini*. (The Italian name, *porcino*, means 'little pig', perhaps because pigs like the mushroom or because young specimens look like fat little piglets.) The flavour of the white flesh is delicate and musty, particularly intense in those grown in more southerly areas.

When you collect the mushrooms, take hold of the stem near the base and twist from

side to side to ease it away from the mycelium. Do not cut it, as the remaining parts may rot, destroying any future growth in the same spot. Wipe off any dirt and do not wash or peel. Dry the mushrooms whole or in slices, and they will lend extraordinary flavour to soups, stews and pasta sauces. Use young specimens raw, thinly sliced, in salads. Whole mature caps can be grilled, baked or fried.

Ceps dry very well, and there are some good varieties of *funghi porcini* available in delicatessens. To reconstitute them, put the dried ceps in a container and pour over enough hot water to cover. Leave them for 30 minutes, then pick out of the water and use as specified in the recipe. Retain the soaking water as this will be very flavourful, but strain it through a fine sieve first to get rid of any sand or grit.

RISOTTO CON PORCINI

CEP RISOTTO

Risotto is one of the classics of Italian food. It has now been adopted by the entire world, and although it's not difficult to prepare, you have to understand the subtle differences in using various ingredients and techniques. You need good rice, butter and Parmesan. If any of the ingredients is not of good quality, then the result will not be a proper risotto. For this recipe it's best to use fresh ceps.

SERVES 4

350g (12 oz) fresh ceps, cleaned
1.5 litres (2¾ pints) very good chicken or
  vegetable stock, well seasoned
100g (3½ oz) unsalted butter
1 onion, finely chopped

325g (11½ oz) vialone nano or carnaroli risotto
  rice
100g (3½ oz) Parmesan cheese, freshly grated
2 tbsp finely chopped fresh parsley
salt and pepper to taste

Slice the ceps finely. Keep the stock on a gentle boil next to your risotto pan.

Put 85g (3 oz) of the butter and the onion into the pan and gently fry until the onion is soft. Add the unwashed rice and stir to coat all the grains with fat. Add the first ladle of hot stock, which will be absorbed almost instantly, and stir. Add a second ladleful and stir until absorbed again. Continue in this way until all the stock has been added to the rice. Now add the ceps and continue to stir and cook, adding more liquid as necessary. After 17 minutes, taste a spoonful of the mixture to see if the rice is *al dente* enough for you. The texture should be quite glutinous, but not 'soupy'.

Now add the rest of the butter, the grated cheese and the parsley. Stir to mix and adjust the seasoning if necessary. Serve immediately.

funghi

PAPPARDELLE CON PORCINI

PAPPARDELLE WITH FRESH CEPS

Pappardelle is a larger version of tagliatelle, which can be bought ready-made or prepared at home yourself. Its combination with ceps in the autumn is a must, or indeed with hare (see page 190). Because ceps grown in Britain are sometimes less flavoursome than their continental counterparts, I use a few dried *funghi porcini* in this recipe for extra flavour.

SERVES 4–6

Fresh pasta

400g (14 oz) Italian soft wheat 00 flour or plain white flour, plus extra for dusting

4 medium eggs (or, if you prefer a softer dough, 3 medium eggs plus 1 egg yolk and a little water)

a pinch of salt

Cep sauce

500g (18 oz) fresh ceps, cleaned

1 large onion, finely sliced

100g (3½ oz) unsalted butter

1 garlic clove, finely chopped

25g (1 oz) dried *funghi porcini*, reconstituted (see page 102), chopped

1 tbsp very finely chopped fresh parsley

salt and pepper to taste

To serve

55g (2 oz) Parmesan cheese, freshly grated

To make the pasta, put the flour on a work surface (marble is ideal), make a well in the centre, and break in the eggs. With a fork, incorporate all the egg gradually into the flour. When everything has come together, start to work with your hands until you have a smooth dough. The more you work it the better. Leave to rest for 1 hour, covered with foil, before using.

Take roughly a third of the dough and put on a clean surface dusted with flour. Using a rolling pin, starting from the centre and rotating the dough, try to roll it out to under 2mm (¹⁄₁₆ in) thickness, still dusting with flour to avoid sticking. Roll the sheet of pasta into a tube or cylinder, using a lot of flour, and cut it into ribbons 2.5cm (1 in) wide. (Using the same method you could cut smaller tagliatelle and even smaller tagliolini, or cut large sheets for lasagne or ravioli.) Unroll the ribbons on to a clean cloth and the pasta is ready. It is much easier if you have a pasta machine, which rolls the dough thinly and also cuts it.

To start the sauce, finely slice the cleaned ceps. Fry the onion in the butter, then add the garlic after 5 minutes. Add the drained, chopped dried *porcini* and cook for a further 5 minutes. Add the fresh ceps and stir-fry for 10 minutes. Season with salt and pepper and the parsley. If more moisture is needed in the sauce, then the reserved *porcini* soaking water may be used.

Boil the pasta in plenty of salted water – 1 litre (1¾ pints) per 100g (3½ oz) fresh pasta plus 10g (¼ oz) salt – until *al dente*. If the pasta is fresh, this should take about 4–5 minutes; if dry, then about 6–7 minutes. Drain and mix into the sauce. Sprinkle with the Parmesan and serve.

FINFERLO

CHANTERELLE *Cantharellus cibarius*

My wife Priscilla loves this graceful, highly prized mushroom, and
is much more adept at spotting it than I am when we are out foraging for wild mushrooms
together. Also known as girolle, it appears from summer to late autumn, singly or in groups,
usually in mixed woods, often in moss but occasionally on soil. It grows all over Europe and,
perhaps surprisingly, is common as far north as Scandinavia, but especially in Scotland. The
caps are convex and small at first, but become funnel shaped, up to 8cm (3¼ in) in
diameter, as the mushroom matures. The stem is thick and wide, tapering towards the
base, up to 6cm (2½ in) tall in larger specimens. The colour is a brilliant apricot yellow, and
the smell is faintly reminiscent of apricots as well. The inner flesh is pale yellow, tasting
slightly peppery when raw.

   Ease the mushroom gently from the soil or moss, or cut. Clean by brushing; it will lose
flavour if washed. It is best eaten fresh, but may be kept in the refrigerator for four to five
days, covered with a damp cloth. It does not dry or freeze particularly well, although it is
quite often found dried. Use in soups, stews or sauces or, my favourite, fried in butter and
then added to scrambled eggs.

COLAZIONE DEI TROVAFUNGHI

MUSHROOMS PICKERS' BREAKFAST

Imagine that you have already been in the woods for a few hours, and it is early morning. You have found some wonderful chanterelles, and with luck you already have with you a couple of eggs, some butter, a rasher of bacon and a small frying pan. You need only a couple of good branches of dry wood and a match to organise a delightful, well-deserved break!

SERVES 4 FOR BREAKFAST

200g (7 oz) fresh chanterelles, larger ones cut up

8 medium eggs, beaten

4 bacon rashers, finely chopped

salt and pepper to taste

55g (2 oz) unsalted butter

Clean the chanterelles well, washing if necessary as they can be sandy.

Fry the bacon in the butter in the pan until crisp. Add the chanterelles and stir-fry for 5 minutes. Add the eggs, salt and pepper and cook, stirring as for scrambled eggs, until the desired consistency. Eat immediately with some good bread.

funghi

RAVIOLO APERTO CON FINFERLI E ANITRA

OPEN RAVIOLO OF CHANTERELLES AND DUCK

This recipe was created with some leftovers from a roast duck, but you could use any other game meat. The important point is to pair the meat with some fresh chanterelles for the delicate marriage of flavours.

SERVES 4

200g (7 oz) fresh chanterelles

125g (4½ oz) unsalted butter

1 small onion, finely chopped

2 speck rashers, finely shredded

200g (7 oz) cooked (preferably roasted) duck meat, cut into strips

4 fresh sage leaves

4 bay leaves

1 sprig fresh rosemary

a little freshly grated nutmeg

2 tbsp coarsely chopped fresh parsley

8 × 12cm (4½ in) squares of *Fresh Pasta* (see page 104)

a little olive oil

55g (2 oz) Parmesan cheese, freshly grated

salt and pepper to taste

Clean the chanterelles well.

Melt 100g (3½ oz) of the butter in a pan and fry the onion and speck until golden. Add the duck meat, sage, bay leaves, rosemary and nutmeg. Stir-fry for 5–6 minutes, then discard the herbs. Add the chanterelles to the pan, and cook for a further 10 minutes. Finally add some salt and pepper and the parsley.

Put the fresh pasta sheets into a pan of boiling salted water containing a few drops of olive oil (the only time olive oil need be added, to prevent the large sheets of pasta sticking together), and cook for 3–4 minutes. Drain well.

Spoon a little sauce on to each hot plate, then place a pasta square on top. Put a quarter of the remaining sauce in the centre, then cover with another pasta square. Brush with the remaining butter, which you have melted, and sprinkle the freshly grated cheese on top. Serve immediately.

LEPISTA

WOOD BLEWIT *Lepista nuda*

This beautiful fungus is fairly common in Europe and North America, but I first encountered it when I came to Britain, I never saw it in Italy. When young the fungus is all over blue-violet in colour at first – stem, cap and gills – the cap turning browner as the mushroom ages. The name 'blewit' in English is a corruption of 'blue hat'. The round flat cap can reach up to 12cm (4½–5 in) in diameter, and the stem is fairly short. It can be found from autumn through to early winter in deciduous woods (beech especially) and fields adjacent to woods; occasionally it appears in gardens, liking a warm pile of lawn grass mowings. They grow singly usually, sometimes in small groups, but a close relative, the field blewit (*L. saeva*), grows in 'fairy' rings. (The '*pied bleu*' or 'blue foot' of the French is the cultivated variety of the field blewit. It is available from good shops, but also from supermarkets.)

The smell of a wood blewit is quite pronounced, and this persists after cooking. They must be cooked, as the raw flesh is slightly poisonous. The texture is quite firm, and the flavour faintly nutty and fragrant. I like them best braised in butter, then mixed with fresh chopped chives and lots of seasoning, but they can be used in pies, risottos and sauces. They do not dry well, but can be pickled or frozen.

Pick the whole mushroom from the ground, and scrape off dirt from the base of the stem. Wipe, do not wash. Slice if large.

funghi

PICCIONI IN CASSERUOLA CON LEPISTA

CASSEROLE OF WOOD PIGEON WITH WOOD BLEWITS

The wood blewit's very firm and fragrant flesh makes it one of the most desirable of wild mushrooms. I've seen them on sale in markets in the Midlands, but I always get mine, some wonderful examples, from my friend Timothy Neat in Scotland, which are sent by express delivery.

SERVES 4

600g (1 lb 5 oz) fresh wood blewits

4 wood pigeons, prepared by your butcher

plain flour for coating

6 tbsp olive oil

2 smoked *pancetta* or bacon rashers, cut into strips

1 onion, finely sliced

1 carrot, finely sliced

1 celery stick, finely sliced

100ml (3½ fl oz) red wine

1 tbsp juniper berries

4 bay leaves

stock or water if necessary

salt and pepper to taste

Clean the blewits, and slice if large. Season the pigeons both inside and out, then dust them with flour. Put them into a hot pan with the oil and *pancetta,* and fry on both sides until golden. Remove from the pan and set aside.

Put the chopped vegetables into the same pan and fry until soft, about 10 minutes. Add the wine, salt and pepper and heat to let the alcohol evaporate.

Put the pigeons, breast side down, into a large casserole dish with the mushrooms, juniper berries, bay leaves, vegetables and their juices. Put on the lid and leave to stew on a gentle heat on top of the stove for half an hour. Should the mushrooms not exude enough moisture, then add a little stock or water.

After half an hour, turn the pigeons round so that they are breast side up, and cook for another half hour. For the last 10 minutes, remove the lid to thicken the sauce. Remove the bay leaves and serve the pigeons with their blewit sauce. A good accompaniment would be boiled rice or wet polenta.

funghi

LEPISTA E FINFERLI SALTATI

WOOD BLEWIT AND CHANTERELLE SAUTÉ

The wood blewit is the mushroom that signals the end of the fungi season, appearing until about the end of November in Britain. Its texture reminds me of the St George's mushroom, which is the first of the season in April.

SERVES 4

300g (10½ oz) fresh wood blewits

300g (10½ oz) fresh chanterelles

1 garlic clove, very finely chopped

85g (3 oz) unsalted butter

2 tbsp coarsely chopped fresh parsley

salt and pepper to taste

Clean the mushrooms carefully.

Fry the garlic briefly in the butter, then add the mushrooms and stir-fry for 10 minutes. Season to taste. Just before serving, add the parsley and mix well. Serve as a side dish, or as a starter with some *bruschetta*.

funghi

PLEUROTO

OYSTER MUSHROOM *Pleurotus ostreatus*

One of the few wild mush-rooms that has been found suitable for cultivation, the oyster is named because of the shape and colour of its cap. It is oval, 6–14cm (2½–5½ in) across, with loosely frilled edges that vaguely resemble those of an oyster shell, and its blue-grey colour when young is also faintly oyster-like. The cap becomes pale golden-grey brown when mature. They can be found from early summer if it is warm until the first frosts of late autumn, sometimes all year round. The mushrooms grow together laterally (like bracket fungi) on fallen trees and stumps (mostly beech) or at the base of unhealthy trees, their mycelia breaking through the bark. They are often found on elm trees felled or killed by Dutch Elm disease, and they will grow on until the trees completely disintegrate. Oyster mushrooms are cultivated in Japan and China.

A close relative of the oyster is *P. cornucopiae* which, although sharing many *Pleurotus* characteristics, is cornucopia-like, rather like a pale horn of plenty.

Cut off at the base where they attach to the wood, and inspect larger ones carefully as there may be maggots in the stems. Cut off the stem parts if at all unsure. Brush to clean, but do not wash, as they will absorb too much water. Oysters do not have much flavour – wild are superior in this respect to cultivated – but their texture is good. Sauté them with garlic, butter and olive oil, deep-fry them in a batter or egg and breadcrumbs, and use them in stir-fries and soups, or even grill them. The photograph on page 115 shows a mixture of fried and grilled oyster mushrooms.

Oysters can be preserved, but do not freeze or dry well.

PLEUROTI FRITTI

OYSTER MUSHROOMS FRIED IN BREADCRUMBS

Italians adore fungi, *funghi porcini* in particular, when coated and fried in breadcrumbs. It is possible to make this dish with a mixture of fungi, but it is best with oyster mushrooms because, being flat, they produce little cutlets.

SERVES 4

16 large oyster mushrooms, cleaned

plain flour for coating

2 medium eggs, beaten

1 garlic clove, very, very finely chopped

1 tbsp finely chopped fresh parsley

olive oil for frying

dried breadcrumbs for coating

1 lemon, quartered

salt and pepper to taste

Take the mushrooms and one by one dip them into the flour, shaking off any excess. Season the beaten eggs, and mix in the garlic and parsley.

Pour 1cm (½ in) of olive oil into a large shallow pan over heat. Dip the mushrooms into the egg mixture first, then the breadcrumbs, then fry in the hot oil until golden on both sides. Serve immediately with a lemon quarter.

PLEUROTI ALLA GRIGLIA

GRILLED OYSTER MUSHROOMS

By using large specimens of this wild and delicious fungus, you may find extra protein hidden in the middle of them, for larger oysters will probably have little maggots inside (cut off the stem if so).

SERVES 4

12 large oyster mushrooms, cleaned

Marinade

8 tbsp olive oil

1 garlic clove, very finely chopped

2 tbsp very finely chopped fresh parsley

1 chilli, very finely chopped

juice of 1 lemon

salt to taste

Make the marinade an hour beforehand to allow the flavour to develop. To do this, combine all the ingredients and leave to stand in a bowl.

Prepare a charcoal grill, and when it is hot, brush each mushroom with the marinade and grill for 5–6 minutes on each side. Baste throughout the cooking, and serve hot accompanied by toast or a wonderful steak.

funghi

SPUGNOLA/MORCHELLA

MOREL *Morchella esculenta*

This very valued but fairly rare mushroom belongs to the mushroom

category known as ascomycetes (which includes the truffle). Its spores are stored in sacs in the sponge-like pits of its cap rather than in gills or pores. These spores are ejected violently when the mushroom is mature.

The morel is one of the first mushrooms to appear in the spring, and there are various types, only a few of which are edible, among them *M. esculenta* and *M. elata*. They tend to grow in countries where there is a well-regulated seasonal cycle of cold/mild/hot/mild – so they are best, and most appreciated, in Italy, France, Switzerland and, perhaps surprisingly, the American Mid-West. Morels favour sandy soil with underlying chalk, and are found in open woodland, around woods, in pastures, orchards and waste land, quite often appearing on land that has been burned. The conical sponge-like cap is tan to pale brown in colour (*M. elata* is darker than *M. esculenta*) and the stems are pale off-white, slightly more swollen towards the base. They normally grow up to 9cm (3½ in) in height, but in America – where else? – they can be found up to 25cm (10 in)!

Pluck whole from the ground or cut the stem, and scrape the stem clean of sand and dirt. Brush the cap clean as much as possible, and try to avoid washing. Morels should be cooked because, when raw, they can be slightly indigestible. Their flavour is pleasant, as is their texture. Use them as a garnish after sautéing gently in butter, and they are delicious in cream sauces, omelettes, with chicken, beef and fish dishes. They dry very well, and after reconstitution, I find they taste extraordinarily like bacon!

funghi

ROGNONCINI SALTATI CON SPUGNOLE

CALF'S KIDNEY SAUTÉED WITH MORELS

This is a much-loved dish in my restaurant, where I use dried morels from Tibet. In that part of the world, lots of morels are collected after cold winters, and then they are dry-smoked. Just like *funghi porcini*, when soaked in water they reconstitute, returning to their original size.

SERVES 4

30g (1¼ oz) dried morels, or 150g (5½ oz) fresh

500g (18 oz) calf's kidney, trimmed of fat

plain flour for dusting

55g (2 oz) unsalted butter

55g (2 oz) speck, cut into strips

2 garlic cloves, finely chopped

50ml (2 fl oz) sherry

2 tbsp coarsely chopped fresh parsley

salt and pepper to taste

Soak the dried morels in water for 30 minutes. Meanwhile, cut the kidney into thin slices and soak in water for 30 minutes. Drain both morels and kidney and pat dry with kitchen paper, reserving a little of the water from the morels. Dust the kidneys with flour.

In a casserole dish melt the butter, then add the kidney slices and stir-fry for 4 minutes. Add the speck, garlic and the morels, fresh or reconstituted dried. Stir-fry for 6–8 minutes then pour in the sherry and the reserved morel water and cook to allow the alcohol to evaporate. Add the parsley and some salt and pepper, then serve immediately with buttered potato purée or lemon rice with butter and Parmesan.

funghi

MORCHELLE RIPIENE

STUFFED MORELS

Ideally you want to use fresh morels all the same size for this dish. It is possible to use dried morels, but fresh give the best results. The French like to stuff them with *foie gras*, but I think this is too rich. If you are vegetarian you can omit the sweetbreads – the result will be just as delicious. Serve as a starter on or with bread, or as a main course with boiled rice.

SERVES 4

12 large fresh morels, up to 8cm (3¼ in) long, or 24 smaller ones, up to 5cm (2 in) long

100g (3½ oz) calf's sweetbreads, trimmed of gristle and nerves

85g (3 oz) unsalted butter

25g (1 oz) dried *funghi porcini*, reconstituted (see page 102), chopped

4 spring onions, finely chopped

1 tbsp brandy

2 tbsp finely chopped fresh parsley

2 medium egg yolks

2 tbsp balsamic vinegar

4 tbsp double cream

salt and pepper to taste

Make sure the morels are sand free, and then cut the stem off at the bottom of the cap. Chop this stem finely and reserve. Blanch the sweetbreads in boiling water for 10–15 minutes. Drain well, then coarsely chop.

Put 25g (1 oz) of the butter in a pan, then fry the *porcini,* onion and sweetbread until the latter is pale to white in colour – about 6–8 minutes. Mix together with the chopped morel stalks, brandy, half the parsley and salt and pepper to taste. Stir-fry for a little longer, then cool. Bind with the egg yolks, and stuff each large morel with the mixture, taking care not to break them.

Sauté the morels in the remaining butter for 10–15 minutes, turning carefully. Just before they are ready, add the balsamic vinegar and cream to the pan and cook briefly into a buttery sauce. Sprinkle with the remaining parsley and serve immediately.

funghi

LINGUA DI BUE

BEEFSTEAK FUNGUS *Fistulina hepatica*

You might think wild mushrooming was all about scanning the
ground for booty, but with bracket fungi such as beefsteak, you have to look upwards. For
the beefsteak fungus is a tree dweller, preferring to form on and parasitise oaks and sweet
chestnuts. It grows out from the stump or tree trunk, looking rather like a bracket or shelf,
and although usually found near the base of the tree, it can occur at a higher level. It is
broadly tongue-shaped and tongue-coloured, which has led to its alternative name in
English of 'ox tongue' – and indeed to its German and Italian names, *Ochsenzunge* and
lingua di bue respectively. It can grow from 10–25cm (4–10 in) across, and from 2–6cm
(¾–2½ in) thick. As with many parasitic fungi, the beefsteak can lead to the destruction of
a tree, but in the case of oaks, there is a side benefit: the rot the fungus causes creates a
deeper, richer coloration of the wood which is highly prized by furniture-makers.

The season for beefsteak is late summer to early autumn, and it grows all over Great Britain
and Europe. It is red in colour when young, becoming more orange-yellow as it matures.
The fungus should smell pleasant, but the taste of its yellow-pink flesh is quite sour when raw.
Cut it from the tree, leaving behind the 'stalk'. To clean, simply brush, perhaps cutting away
a little more of the flesh where it attached to the tree. The inner flesh of the cut fungus is
veined rather like steak, thus its common name and an alternative country name of 'poor
man's meat'. When cooked, the flesh turns darker, but it is succulent and meaty. Use it, cut into
chunks, in stews as an accompaniment to fatty or rich foods such as sweetbreads or brains.

funghi

LINGUA DI BUE ALLA CREMA

BEEFSTEAK FUNGUS WITH DILL AND CREAM

I am afraid that I have already given this recipe in another book, but I find it so ideal that few other ways of cooking it would produce a better result. It can be used as part of a mixed sautéed fungi dish, or in salads. It is wonderful if accompanied by good toasted bread.

SERVES 4

600g (1 lb 5 oz) beefsteak fungus

1 garlic clove, finely chopped

55g (2 oz) unsalted butter

4 tbsp double cream

2 tbsp coarsely chopped fresh dill

salt and pepper to taste

Clean the beefsteak well, then slice finely.

Fry the garlic in the butter for a few minutes, then add the sliced beefsteak and stir-fry for 7–8 minutes. Add the cream, dill, salt and pepper, and cook for a further 2–3 minutes. Serve immediately.

LINGUA DI BUE FRITTA

FRIED BEEFSTEAK FUNGUS

The beefsteak's special look, taste and texture make it suitable for only a few recipes. You can prepare as below and then combine it with other mushrooms if desired for a *fritto misto*, or eat by itself.

SERVES 4

800g (1¾ lb) beefsteak fungus

3 medium eggs, beaten

1 tbsp very finely chopped fresh dill (optional)

plain flour for coating

dry breadcrumbs for coating

olive oil for shallow-frying

salt and pepper to taste

lemon wedges to serve

Clean the beefsteak, then slice, not too thinly.

Season the beaten egg mixture, and mix in the dill (if using). Dip the slices of beefsteak firstly in the flour, then the egg and lastly in the breadcrumbs. When they are well coated, shallow-fry in the hot oil until golden and crisp, a few minutes only. Serve hot with the lemon wedges.

funghi

TRICOLOMA/MARZOLINO

ST GEORGE'S MUSHROOM *Tricholoma gambosum*

This very special small mushroom gets its English name because, in Britain, it is found traditionally on or around St George's Day, 23 April. (In fact, it is usually better a week or so later.) In Italy it is known as *marzolino* because it usually appears in *Marzo*, or March, a little earlier than in Britain. It is the first mushroom of the year to be enjoyed. It is found in grass on roadsides or on pastureland, occasionally on the edges of woods, but the best place to find it is on racecourses where the earth hasn't been cultivated. This allows the mycelium to grow in circles, expanding each year to make larger circles. A very revealing clue is the colour of the grass, which is much greener than the surrounding growth. This is the effect of the mycelium underneath (why, I don't know). It is easy to spot these circles: the mushroms will form the rings one after the other, so called 'fairy rings' because it was thought this wonder of nature was due to the dancing of fairies.

The cap can measure from 5–15cm (2½–6 in) across, and is white; the gills are also white; the stem is slightly chubby, becoming thinner with age. The flesh is soft, and has a mealy smell and taste. Pull the mushroom carefully from the mycelium, and brush clean of soil and grass. Trim the ends of the stems. Slice or use whole – they are good sautéed in butter or olive oil with a little garlic. They can also be pickled.

TRICOLOMA SOTT'OLIO

PICKLED MUSHROOMS

In Italy almost everyone pickles some mushrooms to be eaten as *antipasto*, possibly with some slices of salami or Parma ham, during the Christmas festivities. The mushroom most frequently used is the cep or *porcino* but the St George's mushroom, with its solid and thick flesh, is also excellent.

Preserved mushrooms are safe to keep so long as you ensure that the preserving agent – salt or vinegar – has penetrated the interior of the mushroom. Great care should be taken because of the danger of botulism.

FILLS 2 × 500G (18 OZ) JARS

1.5kg (3 lb 5 oz) St George's mushrooms (cleaned weight)

2 litres (3½ pints) white wine vinegar

20g (¾ oz) salt

6 cloves

6 bay leaves

500ml (18 fl oz) olive oil

Prepare 2 sterilised 500g (18 oz) jars. Put the vinegar in a stainless-steel pan with 1 litre (1¾ pints) water, the salt, cloves and bay leaves. Bring to the boil, then add the mushrooms and cook for 15 minutes, longer if they are large. Using a clean slotted spoon, transfer the mushrooms to a clean cloth to cool and dry.

Wearing rubber gloves (to avoid bacteria), transfer the mushrooms to the jars and then cover completely with olive oil. Press them down tightly, and make sure they are all submerged. You may use the bay leaves for decoration in the jars. Close the lids very tightly and keep until required, for up to a year.

funghi

TRICOLOMA SALTATI IN PADELLA

ST GEORGE'S MUSHROOM SAUTÉ

As usual in mid April, I was impatiently waiting to be summoned to Birmingham, where two of my mycological friends, the Batemans, live. They watch the fields very carefully to see when the magic circles of green grass contain any St George's mushrooms. My trip in the year 2000 didn't disappoint, and as you can see from the photograph on page 121, our booty was really quite something – and was eaten for breakfast!

SERVES 4 FOR BREAKFAST

500g (18 oz) St George's mushrooms, cleaned

55g (2 oz) unsalted butter

1 garlic clove, thinly sliced

2 tbsp coarsely chopped fresh parsley

salt and pepper to taste

Cut the biggest mushrooms in halves or quarters.

Melt the butter in a frying pan, add the garlic and fry for a couple of minutes. Add the mushrooms and sauté for another 10 minutes. Season with salt, pepper and the parsley, and decorate with chopped fresh wild garlic, if you like. Serve with toast.

TARTUFO

TRUFFLE *Tuber spp*

I have been passionate about fungus-hunting since I was about seven or eight, when a professional truffle-hunter friend of my father's, Giovanin, took me on a hunt with him. The elation when we found a truffle (or rather, when Giovanin's mongrel, Fido, did), was to remain with me for years thereafter. In fact I still feel as excited as a seven-year-old when I spot a haze of flies under an oak tree, a good hint as to the presence of a truffle.

The truffle we found that day was the white truffle of Italy, *Tuber magnatum*, but two others are as highly esteemed – the black Périgord truffle (*T. melanosporum*) and the summer truffle (*T. aestivum*). Truffles are ascomycetes, and they all grow underground rather than above ground, in association with certain trees – *T. magnatum* with oak, hazel, poplar and beech, *T. melanosporum* with oak, and *T. aestivum*, the only one found in England, usually with beech, occasionally with oak.

The white truffle is cream to brown in colour, and can weigh up to 500g (18 oz). The season is from late September through to late January. It is found mostly near Alba in Piedmont, but also in Tuscany and even in Calabria. I shave it on a mandolin over omelettes, pasta and risotto. I also pop a truffle into a container with eggs to flavour the eggs. The black truffle is famous for its Périgord connection, but can also be found in parts of Italy, from mid November to March. At most it weighs 100g (3½ oz). It has a rough black skin made up of hundreds of 'warts'. The cut slices are marbled brown with white veins, which disappear on cooking. They can be eaten raw, but are usually used with cooked food – under the skin of a roast chicken, in pâtés, with *foie gras*. The summer truffle looks rather like the black truffle, but with rougher 'warts'. It rarely weighs more than 300g (10½ oz). It appears between June and November, sometimes throughout the winter.

Scrub truffles well with a wire brush, never wash them. Shave and use raw preferably. Keep in the fridge (in a covered container, or *everything* will taste of truffle!) for a maximum of seven days for the white, fourteen days for the black. Try to use as soon as you can, for once a truffle becomes wet and soggy it must be thrown out – and that could be expensive…

funghi

TAGLIOLINI AL TARTUFO NERO

TAGLIOLINI WITH BLACK TRUFFLE

It is difficult to describe how wonderful the combination of truffles and pasta is. This particular recipe is one of the simplest, but it's also very sophisticated. If made using the very expensive white truffle from Alba, this dish will then probably be the best in the world! To reinforce the flavour, you could perhaps drizzle over a few drops of truffle oil …

SERVES 4

85g (3 oz) black truffle

85g (3 oz) unsalted butter

a few drops of truffle oil (optional)

500g (18 oz) fresh tagliolini, or 450g (1 lb) good-quality dried

55g (2 oz) Parmesan cheese, freshly grated

salt and pepper to taste

Clean the truffle well, then cut into minute cubes.

Melt the butter in a pan, then add the truffles and 2 tbsp water. Let this cook very slowly for 10 minutes. Add salt, pepper and the truffle oil (if using).

Cook the pasta in boiling salted water for 4 minutes if fresh, and 6 minutes if dried. Drain, reserving 4–6 tbsp of the cooking water, then transfer to the sauce in the pan. Add the reserved cooking water, along with the Parmesan, and mix well. You could garnish with a few slices of truffle before serving.

funghi

TROTA AL TARTUFO

UMBRIAN TROUT WITH TRUFFLES

This dish is a speciality of Umbria, especially of the Nera River valley, where the wild trout are of excellent quality. It combines two local ingredients in a wonderful marriage of flavours.

SERVES 4

100g (3½ oz) summer or winter truffle

4 × 300g (10½ oz) rainbow or brown trout, gutted and cleaned

1 onion

1 celery stick

1 carrot

1 *bouquet garni*

6 tbsp Umbrian extra virgin olive oil (or equivalent)

1 garlic clove, coarsely sliced

salt and pepper to taste

Clean the truffle carefully then, at the last minute, cut it into minute cubes.

In a suitable pan, make a *court-bouillon* with enough boiling water to cover the trout, along with the onion, celery, carrot and *bouquet garni*. Add the trout and poach for about 12–15 minutes, depending on size. You could also steam the fish if you preferred.

In a separate pan heat the olive oil, and add the garlic followed by the truffle. Gently fry for 10 minutes, then discard the garlic. Season the 'truffled' oil to taste with salt and pepper.

Bone the trout, and then transfer the fillets to hot plates. Pour over the truffle sauce. If you have a small amount of truffle to spare, then it may be sliced very thinly and used to garnish the fish. Serve with boiled potatoes.

funghi

ORECCHIO DI JUDA

JUDAS EAR MUSHROOM *Auricularia auricula-jude*

This gelatinous fungus, shaped uncannily like an ear, is also known as the jew's ear mushroom. It is common on the trunks and branches of the elder tree, and it is said to have got its name because Judas hanged himself from an elder. The mushrooms can be found all year round, but are particularly frequent in autumn, especially after rain. The outer part of the cap is brown, the curved inside paler, with veins that reinforce the mushroom's resemblance to an ear. This mushroom does not have gills or pores producing spores, as the latter are produced on the surface of the mushroom, and dispersed on to the tree by wind and rain. The judas ear mushroom is closely related to the wood ear or cloud ear mushroom (*A. polytricha*) which is cultivated and dried in China, and lends its jelly-like texture – something the Chinese appreciate more than we in the West do – to many stir-fried and stewed dishes. They also call it the 'black fungus' because it becomes black when dried. They dry very successfully in fact, returning to virtually full size and shape after soaking.

Pick the mushrooms or cut them, and wipe them before cooking. I pick not only the fresh specimens – each lobe growing up to 10cm (4 in) in diameter and 3mm (⅛ in) in thickness – but those that have already dried on the tree. They feel cold and soft, because of their gelatinous texture. And that is the most important element with this mushroom, along with its colour, as it does not have much aroma or flavour. It is used to enrich the look of salads, and to make sauces for pasta and risotto. It stews very well, but do not fry in hot oil for too long, as it literally explodes!

funghi

RISOTTO CON ORECCHIETTE

JUDAS EAR RISOTTO

Because these mushrooms are not particularly flavourful, I have cheated a little and added some dried *funghi porcini*. If you cook the rice *al dente*, as they generally do in Italy, this dish will give an interesting contrast in textures – the 'bite' of the rice contrasting with the gelatinous feel of the mushrooms. Because the mushrooms dry so well, you can make this dish at any time of year.

SERVES 4

200g (7 oz) judas ear mushrooms

10g (¼ oz) dried *funghi porcini*, reconstituted (see page 102)

1.5 litres (2¾ pints) chicken or vegetable stock, well seasoned

3 tbsp good olive oil

1 small onion, finely chopped

350g (12 oz) arborio or other risotto rice

55g (2 oz) Parmesan cheese, freshly grated

25g (1 oz) unsalted butter, cut in cubes

25g (1 oz) fresh flat-leaf parsley, finely chopped

salt and pepper to taste

Wash the fresh mushrooms well, then cut into large strips. Slice the reconstituted dried mushrooms. Bring the stock to a simmer in a saucepan.

Heat the oil in a large pan, add the onion, and fry gently until soft and transparent. Add both types of mushroom, and stir-fry for 5 minutes. Add the rice, and stir to coat each grain with oil. Add the strained *porcini* soaking liquid and stir for a minute, then add the hot stock, a ladleful at a time, stirring continuously. Wait until each ladleful is absorbed before you add the next. After about 15–20 minutes the rice should be cooked *al dente*. Remove the pan from the heat, and add the Parmesan, butter, salt and pepper to taste. Mix well, sprinkle with parsley, and serve immediately.

funghi

INSALATA DI FUNGHI MISTI

MIXED FUNGI SALAD

Every time I return from a fungi hunt, even if I only have a few varied specimens, then it is time to make this exciting salad. It can be eaten as a starter by itself, or can accompany fish dishes or cold roast meats. It may be eaten hot or cold.

SERVES 4

200g (7 oz) each of judas ear mushrooms, oyster mushrooms, wood blewits and chanterelles

500ml (18 fl oz) water

250ml (9 fl oz) strong white wine vinegar

4 bay leaves

8 tbsp extra virgin olive oil

1 garlic clove, finely chopped

1 fresh chilli, finely chopped

2 tbsp coarsely chopped fresh flat-leaf parsley

1 lemon, cut into wedges

salt and pepper to taste

Bring the water and vinegar to the boil in a stainless-steel pan with 1 tsp salt and the bay leaves. Throw the mushrooms into the boiling liquid and cook for 8–10 minutes. Drain and discard the liquid.

Put the olive oil, garlic and chilli into a large pan and fry very briefly. Add the drained mushrooms and toss in the pan over heat to let them absorb the oil and its flavourings. Season to taste with salt and pepper and sprinkle with the parsley. Serve with a wedge of lemon.

funghi

esotici

EXOTICS

IN THIS CHAPTER, I INCLUDE A FEW ITEMS THAT YOU MAY ENCOUNTER, PROBABLY when abroad, and especially around the Mediterranean. In fact, an entirely separate book could be written on this subject. For me, though, they are all normal produce. I decided to call them 'exotic' because they are not freely available in northern Europe.

Capers, juniper berries and pine kernels have become familiar to us in Britain, but only in jars and packets. However, they are cultivated commercially in their countries of origin and can be freely available in the wild as well. In some Mediterranean areas a whole town can be employed in the collection of such foods. For instance, in Puglia, whole families collect wild onions – *lampascioni* – when in season, and then they do the same for wild fungi later on in the year.

But wild foods such as these, particularly the prickly pear which grows all over Europe, are also available from roadside vendors, who eke a small living from selling produce that they have collected. In southern Italy and places like Malta you can still find stalls which offer freshly picked pine cones or prickly pears (or indeed snails). I'm sure it is not possible to survive on such earnings, but I still welcome small traders such as these, because they provide a welcome opportunity to keep one's taste-buds experiencing true flavours and customs of the past.

GINEPRO

JUNIPER BERRY *Juniperis communis*

There are over fifty species of juniper, but the one which yields berries for medicinal and culinary use is *J. communis*. Native to most of the northern hemisphere, it grows widely, adapting itself to different habitats – in Britain, in the cooler north on acid soils, mingling with heather on moorland, and in the warmer south, on exposed chalk downs. It is an evergreen prickly shrub or tree, depending on location; it can appear as a sprawling or prostrate bush in a colony, or as a singular, cylindrical or conical tree up to about 5m (17 ft) in height. The berries – of about 1cm (½ in) diameter – are green at first, turning blue-black or purple during the second or third year. Green and black berries can be seen on the plant at the same time, which has led to one possible explanation of the name 'juniper' – coming from the Latin *juniores*, referring to the continuing presence of new or 'junior' berries. However, it is much more likely that the name is derived from the Latin name *Juniperis* itself (sometimes spelled 'jeniperis'), in common with the French *genièvre*, the Italian *ginepro* and the Dutch *geneva* or *genever*.

The berries, which are tart, fragrant and faintly resinous in flavour, are used – as they are all over Europe – in meat marinades and game dishes. They can actually make milder meats taste a little more 'gamey'. They are also used in pâtés, and in *sauerkraut* (good with fresh cabbage too). The berries are added to liqueurs like Chartreuse, but the most famous drink flavoured by juniper is gin. Some 400 years ago, a Dutch apothecary created *genever* as a diuretic medicine, flavouring a clear spirit with juniper and other 'botanicals' such as angelica, cardamom, coriander and orange peel. I too have developed a drink, a digestif using gin and juniper berries.

esotici

LIQUORE DIGESTIVO DI GINEPRO

GIN AND JUNIPER LIQUEUR

In Italy it is possible to make such a liqueur as this from scratch, because very high proof raw spirit is widely available to buy. Here we have to use a ready-made spirit – in this case, gin – to be reinforced and sweetened. The result makes for an excellent digestif liqueur.

MAKES 1 LITRE (1¾ PINTS)

200g (7 oz) fresh juniper berries, crushed

1 litre (1¾ pints) good gin
    (possibly Tanqueray, with 43% alcohol)

1 bunch fresh mint

2 sprigs fresh rosemary

1 tbsp fresh marjoram

4 fresh bay leaves

1 tsp fennel seeds

rind of 1 lemon and 1 lime

1 slice fresh root ginger

300g (10½ oz) caster sugar or 300g (10½ oz) clear honey

1 small sachet saffron powder

Use a large jar with a tight lid. Pour in all the ingredients apart from the sugar or honey, and leave to macerate for a week.

Dissolve the sugar in a little water then add the saffron and melt over a low heat, until clear and syrupy. Add the syrup to the gin mixture when it is cool and strain everything through a fine sieve. You will have a clear liquid. If using honey, add to the mixture without melting, then strain several times through very, very fine muslin. It will still be a little cloudy, but this doesn't affect the flavour. Pour the intensely flavoured liquid into bottles, and save for an after-dinner tipple. You could also use it for flavouring fruit salads as they would in Italy.

esotici

PINOLO

PINE KERNEL *Pinus spp*

The pine kernel, or pine nut as it is often known, is the edible seed of various species of pine tree. Most of the pine kernels in Europe come from *Pinus pinea*, the Mediterranean stone pine, which ranges from Portugal to the Black Sea. This is the umbrella-shaped tree so typical of the landscape of the coastal regions of Tuscany, Campania and Sicily. Other varieties of pine which produce edible seeds grow in the Far East, Australia, Mexico and North America.

The seeds form within the pine cone. In the countries where pine kernels are harvested and sold, the cones are collected during the winter months, then laid in the sun in the summer to dry and open up, when the seeds can be extracted. At home, a short spell in a hot oven can encourage the cone to open and release the seeds, and I can remember doing this when I was a child. (Which reminds me of the belief that pine cones can act as a barometer: the cones would remain closed if they were cold, would open when warm.) Seeds can only be gathered from the cones of mature trees of at least seventy-five years of age (some pine trees can live for up to 250 years), so commercial cultivation is necessarily small scale (and the price of the kernels correspondingly high). The kernel itself is about 1cm (½ in) long, yellow-white in colour; it is encased in a wooden skin which has to be broken to release the kernel. It tastes sweetly creamy with a touch of turpentine (the resin from another Mediterranean pine is used to make turpentine – and the Greek wine, *retsina*). The flavour can be enhanced by a brief toast in a dry pan or in the oven. Keep bought pine kernels in the fridge, but use them quickly as their oils can become rancid.

Although the stone pine grows in France, pine kernels feature minimally in French cuisine, but in Spain, Italy and the Middle East they feature in many dishes. Used in stuffings for meat, chicken and vegetables in the Middle East, they also add texture to many pilavs. The Arabic influence on the cooking of southern Italy, particularly Sicily, can be seen in many vegetable dishes which unite raisins and pine kernels. In every cuisine in which pine kernels feature, they are used in cakes and biscuits, but their best known manifestation must be in the Genoan pesto sauce.

esotici

PESTO

BASIL SAUCE

The famous pesto sauce from Liguria is mainly made of basil and pine kernels, with the addition of olive oil, garlic and grated cheese. In Liguria it is mainly used to flavour pasta such as linguine (or *trenette*) or *trofie*, a hand-made twirl of pasta. There are also two further common uses of the sauce. One, which is only found east of Genoa, contains *cagliata*, a sort of junket, while on the western side, towards Savona and Ventimiglia, they cook potatoes and green beans with the pasta before saucing with the pesto.

SERVES 4

50g (1¾ oz) pine kernels

15 fresh basil leaves

4 garlic cloves, coarsely chopped

10g (¼ oz) coarse salt

extra virgin olive oil

60g (2¼ oz) Pecorino or Parmesan cheese, freshly grated

I do actually prefer to make this sauce in a pestle and mortar, because I feel that I can control the finished texture better, but you can use a food processor. The resulting sauce should not be as runny as that which you would put on pasta; nor should it be cooked – just warmed up, with the addition of a couple of tablespoons of water for extra moisture.

Place the pine kernels, basil, garlic and salt in the blender. Add a little olive oil, then blend, adding more oil until a smooth paste is formed. Add the cheese and mix well.

esotici

PIGNOLATA

PINE KERNEL CAKE

The name of this pudding-cake comes from the Italian word for pine kernel, *pinolo* (*pignolo* in Tuscany). *Pignolata* can be rather dry, so it is often accompanied by a glass of Vin Santo or 'holy wine' (so called because it was used by connoisseur priests to celebrate mass). Others say, however, that it originallly came from the Greek island of Xantos.

SERVES 8–10

55g (2 oz) pine kernels

175g (6 oz) unsalted butter, softened

150g (5½ oz) caster sugar

2 large eggs

3 large egg yolks

finely grated zest of ½ lemon

100ml (3½ fl oz) Vin Santo

375g (13 oz) Italian soft wheat 00 flour or plain flour

1 tsp baking powder or 1 packet Lievito Bertolini Vanigliato (the Italian equivalent)

Preheat the oven to 220°C/425°F/Gas 7, and use 25g (1 oz) of the butter to grease a round or square 25cm (10 in) baking dish.

Beat the remaining butter with the sugar until light. Beat the eggs and yolks with the lemon zest and Vin Santo until light and foamy, then add to the butter and sugar mixture. Very gently fold in the flour, sifted with the baking powder, using a metal spoon. When everything is very well blended, put into the greased baking dish, and scatter the pine kernels on top. Bake in the preheated oven for 35 minutes, then leave to cool. Turn out of the dish when cold.

CAPPERO

CAPER *Capparis spinosa*

Capers – *capperi* – are the small immature
flower buds of a perennial spiny (thus '*spinosa*') shrub
native to the Mediterranean. In Italy, France, Spain and
Portugal, it is cultivated, but it also grows wild, spreading
up and over walls, along rocks and roadsides. It can reach
a height of about 1.5m (5 ft), becoming very bushy. Its
leaves are quite fleshy, and the flowers, if allowed to
develop, are large, white and pretty, like wild roses, with
long purple stamens. The smaller the bud, the tastier and
more tender the caper will be, and when cultivated, the
bushes are carefully picked each day, an expensive process
which is reflected in the price of the best and smallest
capers. The fruit of the bush can be eaten as well, known
here as caperberries – *cuncunci* – which come, when

pickled, attached to a vestigial stalk. These are larger, sometimes as large as an olive, and are
seedy inside.

Provence is where the best French capers grow, but it is Sicily and two nearby small
islands – Lipari and Pantelleria – that produce Italy's finest. Capers and caperberries need
to be pickled in order to develop their characteristic flavour. This is done either in white
wine vinegar, brine or dry salt. I like the salted best. Whether home-pickled or bought,
salted capers must be soaked in fresh water for about 20 minutes before use, to get rid of
excess salt. Drain them well thereafter.

I use capers in many ways – on pizzas, in white and other sauces (particularly that for veal,
tonnato), in salads (very good with tomatoes), on pasta in Sicilian sauces, with meat and
lots of fish dishes. Capers contribute to three classic French sauces – *tartare, rémoulade*
and *ravigote*, and also appear in the southern speciality, *tapenade*.

If picking from the wild, shake away any ants or other wildlife, and check the capers for
holes which could indicate unwelcome squatters! Detach the closed-up bud and smaller
fruits with your fingernails. Never detach the top shoot or bud, as this must be allowed to
go on growing. And be careful about identification. A caper spurge (*Euphorbia lathyrus*)
looks very similar, but is extremely toxic.

esotici

PASTA DI CAPPERI, OLIVE E MANDORLE

CAPER, OLIVE AND ALMOND PASTE

This paste is easy to prepare and highly versatile. Not only can you spread it on little *crostini*, but it is also essential as an addition to sauces, soups or some pasta dishes. Use salted capers, as they are much richer in flavour.

It is better to blanch the almonds in hot water for a few minutes and then peel them, as this makes it much easier to then reduce them to a pulp.

MAKES ABOUT 500G (18 OZ)

100g (3½ oz) large salted capers, prepared (see page 139)

200g (7 oz) shelled whole almonds (see above)

200g (7 oz) pitted green olives

8 tbsp extra virgin olive oil

Put the almonds into a food processor and blend them to a pulp. Add the olives, capers and olive oil and blend further to make a fine paste. Transfer to an airtight jar.

If you wish to use this as a sauce for pasta, boil the pasta, drain it, then add freshly grated Pecorino cheese and some of the paste which has been diluted with a little of the pasta cooking water.

SALSA DI CAPPERI PER VITELLO TONNATO

CAPER SAUCE FOR VEAL

This sauce is traditionally eaten with very thinly sliced cooked veal. Its vital ingredient is capers, which are combined with *cornichons* (tiny gherkins), tuna and mayonnaise. The sauce is also very tasty spread on *crostini*.

SERVES 4

100g (3½ oz) salted capers, prepared (see page 139)

100g (3½ oz) small pickled gherkins, coarsely chopped

300g (10½ oz) good tuna in olive oil, drained

300g (10½ oz) mayonnaise, freshly made

salt and pepper to taste

Put the capers and gherkins into a blender and then blend to a pulp. Add the tuna and blend again. Next mix in the mayonnaise, and season to taste. The sauce is ready!

esotici

FICO D'INDIA

PRICKLY PEAR *Opuntia ficus-indica*

I'll never forget seeing a woman in Ischia, posing for a photograph of her picking prickly pears. Before I could warn her, she grabbed one of the fruits, and her screams thereafter seemed endless. For these small red, orange and yellow fruits of the *Opuntia* cactus are coated in tiny tufts of bristles which, when they enter the skin, cause intense pain and are very difficult indeed to extract. However, I've seen roadside prickly pear vendors in southern Italy who seem to be immune to the barbs: with bare hands and armed only with a knife, they peel the fruit nonchalantly and hand you the succulent orange-red flesh – usually on a freshly picked mulberry leaf.

Also known as the Indian or Barbary fig or pear, cactus pear or tuna fig, the prickly pear was first introduced by the Spaniards from South America to Europe where it spread happily throughout all the warm countries of the Mediterranean. It can be found in South Africa, India and Australia as well, in some places actually becoming a pest. The cactus grows up to 3–4m (9–12 ft) high, and its 'branches' are fat, plate-like pads, along the edges of which the fruit form.

Prickly pears are cultivated in Central America and the southern USA, and in parts of Europe (particularly Sicily), but they are commonly seen wild as well – actually as an informal 'hedging' around fields in places such as Malta. When picking, do so carefully, wearing sturdy gloves. To peel, use a knife and fork. Spear the fruit on the fork, and top and tail with the knife. Make a cut lengthways, not too deeply, then peel back the skin with the blade of the knife. The flesh is pulpy, with a plethora of little edible seeds. The flavour is very bland and delicate, and reminds me a little of melon. Some citrus juice will help it along. Serve prickly pear raw as a dessert fruit, in slices or whole, or in a fruit salad. The pears make a good jelly and can be stewed. The pulp can be puréed for use as a sauce for something like ham, and the flavour and texture of the fruit go particularly well with bland cheeses such as mozzarella or ricotta.

esotici

ZUPPA DI FICHI D'INDIA E PROSCIUTTO DI PARMA

PRICKLY PEAR AND PARMA HAM SOUP

This recipe is derived from my chilled Parma ham and melon soup, but prickly pears and pomegranate makes a delicate flavour alternative. You will have to put up with a little roughage from the pips in both fruits, but this is good for your digestion …

SERVES 4

12 large prickly pears
½ pomegranate
juice of 1 lime
140g (5 oz) thinly sliced Parma ham, cut into strips or 4 passionfruit (the vegetarian alternative)
1 tbsp fresh chervil leaves
salt and pepper to taste

Carefully peel the prickly pears as described on the facing page, then reduce the flesh to a pulp with a fork. Carefully scoop the seeds out of the half pomegranate and discard the skin and yellow pulp (which is very bitter). Add the pomegranate seeds, some salt and pepper and the lime juice to the prickly pear pulp, then chill for an hour.

Just before serving, divide the soup between 4 plates. It will be quite thick. Add a couple of ice cubes to each plate, and then top with the Parma ham slices and chervil leaves. Should the soup be for vegetarians, then omit the Parma ham and replace with the passionfruit pulp and seeds.

esotici

INSALATA DI FRUTTA DI FINE ESTATE

LATE SUMMER FRUIT SALAD

I combined three of the fruits that I can find in the middle of September for this salad – a last memory of summer before the cold of winter arrives.

SERVES 4

4 large prickly pears
2 oranges
1 pomegranate
100g (3½ oz) caster sugar
1 tbsp lemon juice, or 50ml (2 fl oz) Limoncello (a lemon liqueur) if you like

Peel the pears (carefully), then cut into thick slices or wedges. Peel the oranges and cut into membrane-free wedges. Cut open the pomegranate and pick out the fleshy seeds (discard everything else). Put all the fruit into a stainless-steel or ceramic bowl, add the remaining ingredients, and leave to macerate for an hour. Serve well chilled.

esotici

pesce e frutti di mare

FISH AND SHELLFISH

ON READING *THE TIMES* ONE DAY, I LEARNED OF A CARP THAT HAD ACTUALLY been caught thirty-nine times in the previous twenty-five years. The fish, named 'Basil', must be the most successful escapee of the animal world, and he must realise by now that his destiny is to die a natural death! (Only very recently I read that poachers take carp from ponds in parks and public places to sell them as 'decoration' for wealthy pond-owners in the country. There is a real trade in 'poached' carp!) Actually I cannot understand the dubious sporting attitude of catching a fish and then releasing it back into the water. I think that to put the fish quickly out of its misery and then to speed it from hook to table is in fact less hypocritical. But this is purely subjective!

This chapter mainly concerns foods that you can catch yourself, either by fishing in salt or fresh water, or collecting by hand from the rocks on the seashore. Always make sure you are not trespassing. There is an enormous variety of seafood available, and it ranges from shellfish such as limpets and shrimps, crabs and mussels, to several fish, as well as various algae (or seaweeds, not discussed here). Most such hunting trips require no special equipment such as boats or expensive rods – merely stout waterproof footwear, perhaps a net, a sharp knife and a collecting basket. To be successful you will need some knowledge, though, and this cannot be obtained from books alone. It's best to seek advice from experts if you want to become a real wild seafood hunter. But, for anyone who has a taste for the wild, but can't manage to get there, there's always the option of a good fishmonger!

Most of the creatures featured here are naturally available, although some are farmed as well. You must ensure, however, that you gather from unpolluted waters, as many shellfish in particular can absorb toxins. However, of paramount importance with all fish is its freshness: if you have caught it yourself, that won't be in doubt, but do try to use it as soon as possible. If buying fish, look for bright flesh and a firm, not limp, body; rely too on the integrity of your fishmonger. Fish can be frozen at home, but you must monitor it carefully, because domestic freezers are not as efficient as those used in commerce. And always remember that if you have to buy farmed fish, they will probably differ in flavour and texture, due to the life they have led and to their diet.

We should all try to eat some fish and shellfish every week. Seafood represents good protein, which contains less saturated fat than meat, and fish oils are very beneficial to us in a nutritional sense. With a little imagination and knowledge, you can prepare the most wonderful and tasty dishes using fish and shellfish. The recipes here are the result of a lifetime's cooking of seafood, influenced by my childhood and upbringing. As a result, I have to admit that Mediterranean fish taste quite different to me than those from other seas, and would always be my first choice. But that is subjective again! It only remains for me to wish you *'buona pesca'*, good fishing!

MITILI/COZZE

MUSSEL *Mytilus edulis*

The mussel is probably the most
common of shellfish, and is found mostly in
the northern hemisphere, although a large
green-lipped mussel is unique to New
Zealand. The oval, blue-black mussel of
Europe is a bivalve mollusc, which means it
has a hinged double shell (along with clams,
oysters, scallops and cockles). It is rather a
sedentary creature, attaching itself by means
of its 'beard' or byssus to rocks, jetties,
harbour piles, even the hulls of ships, where it
filter-feeds, drawing nutrients from the sea

water. Wild mussels can obviously be found, but great care must be taken to ensure that
they come from unpolluted water, as they are very susceptible to toxins which can be
extremely dangerous when ingested. Most mussels we see these days, though, are cultivated,
a practice which has been in existence since at least the thirteenth century (its formal name
is 'myticulture').

Mussels are plentiful and inexpensive to buy, particularly in autumn and winter. When
bought – usually in 1kg (2¼ lb) net bags – they should be firmly closed and heavy; if the
shell is open and does not immediately close when tapped, then the mussel may be dead and
must be thrown away. Broken shells should be discarded, as well as mussels which float during
cleaning, or that have not opened after cooking. Before cooking, mussels should be well
washed under cold running water, using a knife to scrape off any barnacles and beards.

I remember well when I was a young boy, going to the southern Italian seaside for holidays,
and eating raw mussels bought from street vendors, which had been freshly opened. Served
with a few drops of lemon juice, I felt as if I were swallowing the essence of the Mediterranean.
Now, forty-five years on, because of pollution and the danger of allergies, one should only eat
them cooked. This is usually done in a little water, wine or cider, with some shallot, parsley
and garlic, sometimes chilli; toss them in a covered pan over a high heat, and they will open
and be ready to eat within minutes. I also wrap them in a savoury coating and deep-fry them,
or sprinkle them with garlicky breadcrumbs and bake them.

COZZE GRATINATE

MUSSEL GRATIN

These mussels are ideal as an *antipasto*. They can be served warm or cold.

SERVES 4 AS A STARTER

1kg (2¼ lb) mussels

4 tbsp extra virgin olive oil or 85g (3 oz) unsalted butter

1 garlic clove, finely chopped

2 tbsp finely chopped fresh flat-leaf parsley

2 tbsp dried breadcrumbs

juice of 1 lemon

salt and pepper to taste

Clean the mussels very well (see page 149). Preheat the oven to 200°C/400°F/Gas 6. Place the mussels in a lidded pan with a few tbsp of water and bring to the boil. Cook until all the mussels are open, shaking the pan every so often (about 5 minutes). Let the mussels cool, then remove the top half shell. Loosen the mussel flesh in the remaining half shell. If they have shrunk too much, put 2 mussels in each half shell.

If using butter instead of olive oil, then mix this with the chopped garlic and parsley. Line the mussels up on a baking tray and, if using the garlic butter, just smear it on top, then sprinkle with the breadcrumbs. If using the oil, mix it with the garlic, parsley and breadcrumbs and sprinkle on top of the mussels. Season, and bake for 5 minutes in the preheated oven until the breadcrumbs are golden and crisp. Squeeze over the lemon juice and serve.

COZZE DEL PESCATORE

FISHERMEN'S MUSSELS

In every coastal town or village in Italy you can find a similar dish.

SERVES 4

1.5kg (3 lb 5 oz) mussels

6 tbsp extra virgin olive oil

1 large garlic clove, finely chopped

½ tsp cayenne pepper or chilli pepper

2 tbsp finely chopped fresh flat-leaf parsley

100ml (3½ fl oz) dry white wine

salt to taste

Clean the mussels well (see page 149). Heat the oil in a large lidded pan, and briefly fry the garlic and cayenne or chilli pepper. Add the parsley, wine and mussels then cover with the lid. Whilst holding the lid, shake the pan to allow the mussels to open properly. After 5 minutes' cooking time, make sure that every mussel is open. (Discard any that are still shut.) Season to taste. Transfer to a serving bowl, pouring over the sauce, and serve with crusty bread.

SALMONE SELVATICO

WILD SALMON *Salmo salar*

The two things I might envy the wild salmon for are its agility in

jumping up waterfalls of considerable height (the word 'salmon' comes from the Latin for 'leap'), and its 'memory', that enables it to return to its river of birth, even after several years' absence.

Like the eel, the salmon leads a 'double life'. Young salmon are hatched in fresh-water shallows upstream in the many rivers of northern Europe and North America, and remain there, growing, for a few years. Then they make their way downriver to the sea, adapting from fresh to salt water, before swimming to their ancestral feeding grounds (the locations of which have only fairly recently been discovered). After feeding, fattening and maturing, the grown fish return to their native waters. There they adjust again to fresh water, and swim upstream, overcoming all obstacles, to reach their natal waters in which they in turn will spawn.

I am, naturally, talking about wild salmon which actually represent only about 10 per cent of the salmon sold in Britain and elsewhere. For 90 per cent of the salmon we can get nowadays is farmed. And these fish can vary considerably in quality, which has led to what amounts to a loss of credibility in salmon as a food.

However, the farming of salmon, so long as it is done well, may be of huge benefit in a very specific way. For several years now, wild salmon have been diminishing in numbers, mainly due to pollution and over-fishing. If good farmed salmon is available, this may help to relieve the pressure on wild stocks to a certain extent, enabling them to build up numbers, strength and resistance again, something salmon lovers the world over would be very happy about.

Most Italians are not too familiar with salmon other than smoked, in that the fish are not present in the Mediterranean. But we do import fresh salmon, and we usually grill or poach it – simplicity is best – or flake the flesh into sauces for pasta. I offer a couple of new ideas here.

GNOCCHI DI SALMONE CON SALSA VERDE

SALMON DUMPLINGS WITH GREEN SAUCE

It is quite difficult to invent a new dish using salmon, but I think you will like this one.

SERVES 4

400g (14 oz) wild salmon, boned and skinned
100ml (3½ fl oz) double cream, lightly beaten
4 medium egg whites, lightly beaten
salt and pepper to taste

Sauce

85g (3 oz) unsalted butter
2 tbsp olive oil
2 tbsp each of chopped fresh dill and rocket
1 tbsp freshly grated wild horseradish

To make the *gnocchi,* mince the salmon very finely and pass through a sieve into a bowl sitting on ice. Add some salt and pepper and carefully fold in the cream and egg white. Leave this mixture to chill for a couple of hours.

For the sauce, melt the butter, then mix with the oil, herbs and some salt and pepper to taste.

Bring a saucepan of salted water to the boil. Using a teaspoon, form little *quenelles* in the shape of *gnocchi* (see page 38), and plunge them into the boiling water. Cook until they come to the surface – a matter of seconds – then drain well, and serve immediately with the sauce.

TARTARA DI SALMONE

TARTARE OF WILD SALMON

The 'curing' of the fish here actually ensures that the fish is practically 'cooked' rather than raw. You need to prepare this dish at least 6 hours before eating to allow the flavours to infuse.

SERVES 4

600g (1 lb 5 oz) wild salmon, boned and skinned
6 tbsp extra virgin olive oil
1 tsp Tabasco
1 tbsp finely chopped fresh dill

1 tbsp salted capers, prepared (see page 139), finely chopped
juice of 1 lemon and the grated zest of ½ lemon
salt and pepper to taste

Mince the salmon in a food processor, or – better still – chop very finely with a knife, then mix together with all the other ingredients. Leave to rest (see above), then check for seasoning. Serve with *bruschetta* or toast rubbed with garlic and brushed with olive oil.

PATELLA

LIMPET *Patella spp*

Limpets are single-shelled molluscs which cling to rocks along the coastlines of the world, looking like small pyramids (which has earned them the name in France of *chapeau chinois* or Chinese hat). There are many varieties, but the most frequently seen is *Patella vulgata*, the common limpet, which has a white-grey ridged shell about 6cm (2½ in) in diameter. Limpets behave exactly as their English name suggests, clinging for dear life to the rock, and you will need a very sharp knife with a pointed tip to detach them. And you should try to 'surprise' them, for at the first sign of danger – the approach of a potential predator, or the waves of high tide – its internal muscular foot will intensify the suction against the rock. (It's best to collect when the sea is calm.) But this same foot is also the limpet's means of mobility: when grazing or feeding, usually on young seaweed at night or at high tide, it can often stray up to 1m (1 yd) or so from its 'home base'. It always returns to its original position, though, where it will have eroded its shape into the rock itself, ensuring a perfect, vacuum fit. At low tide, the creature survives because of water retained within the shell.

Limpets have been eaten for centuries – shells have been found in Stone Age middens, or rubbish tips, in the Orkneys. Make sure you collect them from unpolluted waters, as they can absorb toxins. You can actually eat limpets raw, with simply a squeeze of lemon juice. Older specimens can be a bit tough, but they have a very nutty flavour, and are good in seafood stews and soups, and in seafood sauces for pasta.

And don't forget all the other molluscs, both single shelled and bivalves. When you are searching for limpets, you could easily come across mussels (see page 149), cockles, winkles or whelks, all of which would add flavour and variety to a stew, soup or sauce. They too need to come from unpolluted waters.

LINGUINE COZZE E PATELLE

LIMPET AND MUSSEL LINGUINE

I will never forget this dish, which I ate in La Cambusa restaurant in Positano. I was staying there, and for three days running, I ate the same pasta dish! Linguine are similar to spaghetti, but flat, and are extremely suitable for most fish sauces, especially this one. The quantities below give a more than generous portion per person.

SERVES 4–6

300g (10½ oz) limpets

700g (1 lb 9 oz) mussels

1 garlic clove, finely chopped

1 small fresh chilli, finely chopped

5 tbsp extra virgin olive oil

2 tbsp dry white wine

1 large tomato, finely chopped

500g (18 oz) linguine

2 tbsp coarsely chopped fresh flat-leaf parsley

salt to taste

Clean the shellfish very well. Boil a large pan of salted water for the pasta.

In a separate pan fry the garlic and chilli briefly in the oil, then add the wine and tomato. Cook for 5 minutes, then add the limpets, followed by the mussels a few minutes later. Put the lid on the pan and continue to cook until all the mussels have opened, a few minutes only. Discard any that remain closed. Remove the shells from the limpets and mussels when they have cooled a little, then return the flesh to the sauce.

Cook the pasta until *al dente*, drain and add to the sauce. Transfer to warm serving plates and sprinkle with the parsley. If wished, you may leave some of the mussels in their shells to garnish.

GRANDE ZUPPA DI MARE

GREAT SEAFOOD POT

If you have been fortunate enough to have collected a great variety of seafood from the rocks, this dish is perfect. The ideal would be to have a few limpets, cockles, mussels, whelks, shrimps, small crabs and some small clams. Accompany this with a nice bottle of white wine, some crusty bread and the company of good friends, and you will feel as if you're in the Mediterranean.

SERVES 6

4kg (9 lb) mixed seafood in their shells

2 garlic cloves, finely chopped

6 tbsp extra virgin olive oil

3 tomatoes, finely chopped

100ml (3½ fl oz) dry white wine

½ tsp fennel seeds

1g sachet of saffron strands, or the equivalent of saffron powder

½ tsp cayenne pepper or chilli pepper

2 tbsp chopped fresh flat-leaf parsley

salt to taste

Prepare the seafood by cleaning and scraping any impurities from the shells, then run them under cold water, discarding any that do not seem very fresh.

In a large pot with a lid, fry the garlic in the oil for a few minutes, then add the tomatoes and the wine. Cook for a few more minutes, then add the fennel seeds, saffron and cayenne or chilli pepper.

Start by adding the limpets or cockles, which require a longer cooking time, and cook until they begin to leave their shells. Then add the clams, crabs, shrimps and lastly the mussels. Stir from time to time, and when the mussels have opened up, the dish is ready. The salt may be added at this stage if you wish, but you may find that the sauce is already very salty.

Just before serving, add the parsley and transfer to large bowls or serving plates, so that the juices can easily be mopped up with bread.

TROTA

TROUT *Salmo trutta*

Although of the same species,

two main types of native trout are found in northern European waters. The sea or salmon trout (sometimes known as *S. trutta trutta*) spends part of its life in salt water, coming in to fresh water to spawn like salmon, and the brown or common trout (sometimes known as *S. trutta fario*) lives entirely in fresh water. There are many subspecies of brown trout worldwide, and the principal differences lie in habitat: the best trout to eat are those that live in fast-moving, cold rivers and streams; the trout that live in reservoirs and lakes are generally

less interesting in flavour. Trout can vary in size and coloration depending on habitat and diet: those in clear chalk streams in the south can be lighter in flesh and skin colour than those in peat-brown, more northerly rivers. Sea trout, which some consider to be superior in flavour to salmon, have silvery skins, again like salmon, and a pink flesh coloured by its shellfish diet. Sea trout, probably again because of diet and habitat, are generally much larger than fresh-water trout.

A trout from California, the rainbow trout (*S. gairdneri*), was introduced to Europe in the late nineteenth century, and it has flourished. Because it is so adaptable, and can tolerate warmer and less pure water than the brown trout, it has been stocked in lakes and reservoirs, and is the trout bred on trout farms.

As Jane Grigson said in her *Fish Book*, 'The best trout, whatever the size, variety or place may be, is the one you catch yourself and eat within an hour to two.' To me this is certainly true, and I well remember catching small (not *too* small) *trotelle* in the local stream when I was a child. We just used to wipe the fish, gut them and then fry them in butter, but many recipes exist in the Italian and European tradition – they can be grilled, baked in paper or foil, or fried then marinated in a sweet and sour marinade, *in carpione*. There is even an Umbrian recipe which marries trout with truffles, *trota al tartufo* (see page 126).

TROTA IN CARPIONE

PICKLED TROUT

In Italy, *in carpione* means a method of frying fish to be eaten cold as an *antipasto*, but it is good as a snack at any time of the day. It may be made with sardines, anchovies, red mullet, herring or eel. I prefer to use the whole fish but if you don't want to deal with bones, then first fillet the trout.

SERVES 4–6

8 small trout, about 150g (5½ oz) each, gutted and cleaned
plain flour for coating
olive oil for frying
salt and pepper to taste

Marinade
2 red onions, finely sliced
8 tbsp olive oil
4 fresh bay leaves
2 garlic cloves, finely sliced
4 tbsp white wine vinegar

Season the trout inside and out, and dust them all over with plain flour. Pour 1cm (½ in) olive oil into a frying pan, and fry the trout until golden brown on each side. Transfer the fish to a ceramic dish, placing them side by side in one layer.

In a separate pan, for the marinade, fry the onion in the olive oil, then add the bay leaves and the garlic. Fry for a few minutes then add the vinegar. Pour over the fish, and leave to cool. Leave to rest for a day or two before eating, by which time the fish will have absorbed all the flavours.

pesce e frutti di mare

TROTA AL CARTOCCIO

BAGGED TROUT

Various dishes are cooked *al cartoccio* in Italy, which means enclosed in a bag made of either paper, foil or pastry. The idea is to steam-cook the food, capturing all the added flavours. You can use this method for meat and pasta, as well as for fish.

SERVES 4

4 large trout, gutted and cleaned

2 lemons, sliced

85g (3 oz) unsalted butter

4 tbsp coarsely chopped fresh flat-leaf parsley

4 wild garlic leaves or 1 garlic clove, finely chopped

4 tbsp chopped fresh fennel herb

salt and pepper to taste

Preheat the oven to 200°C/400°F/Gas 6. Prepare 4 pieces of greaseproof paper large enough to enclose an individual fish when folded over double.

Place 2–3 slices of lemon on each piece of paper. Season the trout inside and out, then stuff each one with little pieces of the butter, parsley, garlic and fennel. Place the fish on top of the lemon slices. Place a little more butter and another 2–3 slices of lemon on top of each fish. Seal the paper to make a parcel by folding the edges together at the top all round. Bake all 4 parcels in the preheated oven for 30 minutes.

To serve, open the parcels and transfer the trout to a hot plate along with their juices.

GRANCIPORRO/GRANCEVOLA

CRAB *Cancer pagarus/Maia squinado*

Many crabs are found throughout the world – some 4,000 it is
claimed – and most are edible, but the two principal varieties eaten in Europe are the edible
or common crab or *granciporro* (*Cancer pagarus*) and the spider or spiny crab or *grancevola*
(*Maia squinado*). The former is the one most commonly seen, and it can grow to over
20cm (8 in) in width. It is red-brown in colour with a smooth oval shell and two powerful
claws, and it turns bright red when cooked. The spider is pink-brown in colour, with a
much rounder, very spiny shell; it is the arrangement of its legs, placed in a curve around
the body, that earn it its spider soubriquet. Its claws are very much smaller than those of
the common crab, and its maximum width is about 20cm (8 in).

Many crabs can be bought already cooked, but if you have found your own, either kill it
yourself or get a fishmonger to kill it for you, or cook it, preferably alive. Poach it in boiling
salted water (150g/5½ oz salt per 3 litres /5¼ pints water) for 15 minutes for the first 500g
(18oz) in weight, and 10 minutes more for each extra 500g (18 oz). Leave to rest in the
cooking water for 15 minutes, which will ensure tender meat. After cooking, break off the
small legs from each side, and the claws. Press on the legless body to separate the top and
bottom shells. Lift off the back top shell, and remove and discard the 'dead men's fingers'.

Then scrape out and retain the roe or
coral (the red-orange eggs) and the
brown meat. Crack open and remove the
wonderful fibrous white meat from the
claws and legs. For some recipes – the
classic dressed crab of Britain – you
should keep the dark meat of the body
and the white meat of the claws separate.
I like these meats simply mixed together,
with the coral if available, and dressed
with some salt, lemon juice, parsley and
a little olive oil. To me it is almost better
than lobster! Larger spider crabs can be
grilled (or boiled) whole, and the flesh
added to a good tomato sauce for pasta.

pesce e frutti di mare

FAGOTTO DI GRANCIPORRO

PARCEL OF CRAB

This lovely starter can be served with the *Rocket Salsa* on page 41.

SERVES 4

Pancakes
150ml (5 fl oz) milk
55g (2 oz) plain flour
1 large egg, beaten
olive oil for frying
salt and pepper to taste

Filling
300g (10½ oz) white and brown crab meat
55g (2 oz) mayonnaise
1 tbsp finely chopped fresh dill
juice of ½ lemon
cayenne pepper

To finish and serve
8 strands of long spaghetti, cooked
Rocket Salsa (see page 41)

To make the pancakes, mix the milk and flour with the beaten egg, then season with salt and pepper. Use to make 4 pancakes, frying the mixture in olive oil in a 20cm (8 in) frying pan.

Mix all the filling ingredients together, adding salt, pepper and cayenne to taste. Place a portion of the mixture in the centre of each pancake, folding the sides over to form a parcel with each. Tie the pancakes with a strand of spaghetti, and then serve with the *salsa*.

ZUPPA DI GAMBERETTI E GRANCIPORRO

CRAB AND SHRIMP SOUP

One imagines that the time to eat this rich and warming soup would be in winter, but it is also excellent served chilled in summer.

SERVES 4

1 × 750g–1kg (1 lb 10 oz–2¼ lb) crab, cooked (see page 161)

150g (5½ oz) shrimps

1 small onion, finely chopped

50ml (2 fl oz) extra virgin olive oil

1 garlic clove, finely chopped

1 fresh chilli, finely chopped

juice of ½ lemon

juice of 1 lime

fish or vegetable stock to taste

150ml (5 fl oz) double cream

4 tbsp chopped fresh coriander leaves

salt and pepper to taste

If you have cooked the crab yourself (see page 161), leave it to cool, then crack the claws and extract the meat with the help of a skewer. Then open the main body and extract the brown and coral meat. Mix all the meat together in a bowl. Cook the shrimps in salted water for 6–8 minutes, then peel and chop roughly.

Fry the onion in the olive oil until transparent, then add the garlic and cook until soft. Add the chilli, lemon and lime juices, crab meat and shrimps. Transfer to a blender and liquidise until smooth. Add stock until you have the consistency you require. Reheat, and season to taste, then add the cream and sprinkle the coriander leaves on top. Serve immediately.

ANGUILLA

EEL *Anguilla anguilla*

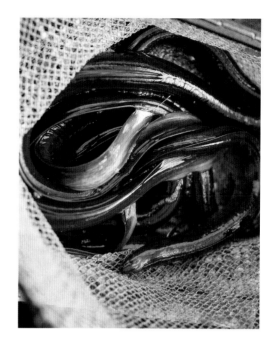

The life-cycle of this snake-like fish

is quite extraordinary. It lives in fresh water until mature, for anything from six to twelve years, then something triggers it to make its way to salt water. Its destination is the area of the Atlantic known as the Sargasso Sea, between Bermuda and Puerto Rico, some 3,000 miles from Europe, a journey which will take them about six months. There the eels spawn and presumably die. The eggs become free-floating, leaf-shaped larvae which drift on the ocean currents, gradually growing until, some three years later in the case of the European eel, they reach their home waters in about March or April. There, as transparent elvers of about 4cm (1¾ in) long, they swim and wriggle their way upstream in fresh water where they will eat, grow, mature, and begin the whole cycle all over again.

Eels were once very much more common than they are now, and changes in sea currents and pollution may have a lot to do with their decline. Sheer greed may be involved as well, for if elvers are caught in quantity at river mouths then mature fish will inevitably become rarer. However, fortunately, a majority of the elver catch these days is being used to stock eel farms. In Italy, for instance, elvers are trapped in artificial lakes when they enter the Po estuary south of Venice, and farmed until they reach maturity.

Eel smokes very successfully and this process somewhat diminishes the fattiness of the flesh. In Italy eels are traditionally eaten fried, grilled and stewed (with tomatoes in Sardinia). Large female eels known as *capitone* are traditionally eaten at Christmas in Rome and further south. Elvers are eaten as well, boiled and seasoned simply, or floured and deep-fried as you would whitebait. In England they cook them with eggs in omelettes, or steam them to make a 'loaf' or 'cake'. In Spain they are cooked in olive oil with chilli and garlic.

Eels should be bought alive, and they are easily dispatched and skinned, but it's perhaps easier if you ask your fishmonger to do it for you (particularly since an eel has a tendency to twitch and wriggle for quite a time after death). The conger eel and moray eel are separate, entirely salt-water, species, which are also eaten.

ANGUILLA ALLA ROMANA

EEL ROMAN STYLE

This is best made using a charcoal grill but an ordinary overhead or oven grill will work just as well.

SERVES 4

1kg (2¼ lb) eels, gutted and cleaned (but not skinned)

Marinade

8 tbsp extra virgin olive oil

5 tbsp white wine vinegar

4 tbsp coarsely chopped fresh mint

3 garlic cloves, sliced

salt and pepper to taste

Cut the eel into 15cm (6 in) chunks, then grill them slowly to allow them to cook through inside, whilst still keeping the skin crisp. You don't need to brush the pieces with oil, as eel is naturally fatty. This will take about 5–10 minutes, depending on the thickness of the eel.

Make the marinade by mixing together all the ingredients. Put the cooked eel into a ceramic container, then pour over the marinade. Leave to infuse for a couple of hours before eating cold, or, if you prefer it warm, you can reheat it in the marinade.

ANGUILLINE NEONATE ALL'AGLIO, OLIO E PEPERONCINO

ELVERS WITH GARLIC, OIL AND CHILLI

The Spaniards are so keen on this dish that they actually make 'false' elvers. These are made from a paste of minced-up fish, which is sculpted to the shape of an elver, with two black eyes and a silver line down the side!

SERVES 4 AS A STARTER

250g (9 oz) elvers, cleaned

12 tbsp extra virgin olive oil

2 garlic cloves, sliced

1 fresh chilli, finely chopped

salt and pepper to taste

Preheat the oven to 200°C/400°F/Gas 6.

Divide all the ingredients between 4 ovenproof ramekin dishes and bake in the preheated oven for 5 minutes, or until the oil bubbles and the garlic is cooked. Serve immediately with fresh bread.

GAMBERO DI FIUME

CRAYFISH *Astacus pallipes/A. fluviatilis*

The crayfish is the fresh-water equivalent of the salt-water common

lobster and spiny lobster (or crawfish), and many varieties exist around the world. Perhaps the most famous are the yabbies and marrons of Australia, and the creatures that are caught in the bayous of the Mississippi delta, and are the speciality of many Cajun restaurants in New Orleans. *A. fluviatilis* used to be common in cold, fast-moving streams in Europe until disease wiped out most of the stock from the nineteenth century onwards. The remaining native populations are now being threatened by the signal crayfish (*Pacifastacus leniusculus*). This was introduced from America to crayfish farms in Sweden because they were immune to the disease, and it has now spread throughout Europe.

Crayfish are both predator and scavenger, living in holes in river and lake banks, coming out to feed at night on live prey or dead or dying fish. They are lobster shaped, but very much smaller, averaging about 10cm (4 in) in length. They have large and strong pincers, but can themselves be prey, to eels, otters and herons, as well as man. They can be caught (in nets and baskets) and eaten from April to October, but are best at the end of summer. The Scandinavians are particularly fond of crayfish, which are found both in the wild and

farmed, and have special festivals to celebrate their brief season. They are usually cooked in water strongly flavoured with dill, and eaten with fresh dill, bread and butter, and accompanied – inevitably – by schnapps and beer. The Americans cook them in gumbos, and the French use their *écrevisses* in mousses and mousselines, and in the famous *sauce Nantua* to accompany *quenelles de brochet* (pike), salmon, sole or chicken. In Italy they are found in little rivers or freshwater ponds, and represent a delicacy, especially in the Po Valley, where they are eaten cooked in tomato sauce and in risottos.

Crayfish must be cooked when alive, and are capable of being kept out of water for a couple of days, so long as they are cool and damp. Cook in boiling water, then shell and remove the thread-like gut, which is bitter.

RISOTTO CON GAMBERI DI FIUME

CRAYFISH RISOTTO

This very elegant risotto requires a little patience in its preparation. It is cooked in two parts: first you must prepare the stock, then the actual risotto itself. Normally dishes with fish do not need any Parmesan sprinkled on them, but because crayfish are so delicate in flavour, the cheese is very complementary.

SERVES 4

30–40 fresh live crayfish

1 onion, finely chopped

100g (3½ oz) unsalted butter

100ml (3½ fl oz) dry white wine

1g packet of saffron strands, or the equivalent of powder (the latter is never so strong in flavour)

350g (12 oz) risotto rice (vialone nano or carnaroli)

85g (3 oz) Parmesan cheese, freshly grated

3 tbsp fresh chervil leaves

salt and pepper to taste

Stock

1 carrot, finely chopped

1 onion, sliced

2 celery sticks, finely chopped

2 bay leaves

To make the stock, fill a pan with 2 litres (3½ pints) water and add the carrot, onion, celery, bay leaves and some salt and pepper to taste. Bring to the boil, then simmer for 30 minutes. Add the crayfish to the stock and cook for 10 minutes. Remove the crayfish and leave to cool. Set aside 4 whole fish to garnish, then remove and retain all the meat from the rest. Crush the crayfish shells with a mallet, then put back into the stock. Cook for about 30 minutes to intensify the stock's flavour. When ready, strain, discarding all the shells and flavourings.

To make the risotto, keep the stock boiling next to the risotto pan, ready to use. Fry the onion in 55g (2 oz) of the butter until soft. Add the wine, saffron and rice, and stir-fry to coat the rice with butter. Start to add the stock ladle by ladle, stirring from time to time until all of the liquid has been absorbed. Do not add more stock until the previous addition has been absorbed. Continue cooking like this for about 15 minutes until you obtain exactly the right balance of moisture – the art of cooking risotto. After 15 minutes add the crayfish meat and cook for a further 4–5 minutes. Test the rice to see if it is *al dente* enough for you.

Remove the pan from the heat, and add the remaining butter, the Parmesan and chervil. Stir well and serve immediately, garnished with the reserved whole crayfish.

pesce e frutti di mare

GAMBERO DI FIUME ALLA SVEDESE

CRAYFISH THE SWEDISH WAY

Crayfish are an excuse for legendary celebrations in Sweden, where they form the main part of a traditional meal. Because of their size, you need to have quite a few to obtain any sort of satisfaction …

SERVES 4

32 fresh live crayfish

1.5 litres (2¾ pints) lager

1 bunch fresh dill

1 tbsp caster sugar

1 tbsp salt

1 tbsp coarsely ground black pepper

Bring the lager to the boil with the dill, sugar, salt and pepper. Add the crayfish and then place the lid on the pan. Cook for 10 minutes, after which the fish should be a beautiful red colour.

Serve on hot plates accompanied by a little of the cooking liquid and, if you want to be really Swedish, with bread and butter, some cheese, and some *Schnapps. Skål!*

pesce e frutti di mare

CARPA

CARP *Cyprinus carpio*

The carp is thought to have originated in China – where it still is a very popular fish to cook – and spread west to Europe in the seventeenth century, reaching America only in the nineteenth century. There are several varieties: the common carp has strong scales all over its body; the mirror carp has fewer scales, in rows; and the leather carp is virtually scale-less. Roach, dace, chub, tench and bream are related – as is the domestic goldfish! The fish prefer to live in still or slow-moving water, which can be quite brackish, and as a result have been used for centuries as a food fish – stocked in monastery and manor-house ponds in the Middle Ages in Britain – and are bred artificially on fish farms throughout the world. They can live up to fifty years (there are age rings on the scales), and can reach up to 20kg (44 lb) in weight. Carp are bottom feeders, usually eating plankton, so can taste quite muddy depending on habitat (soak in brine or vinegared water to counter this). One variety of carp eats grass, so has been introduced to European rivers and ponds to help control weeds.

To prepare carp, soak as above if muddiness is suspected, then scale if necessary. Remove the gills, and clean thoroughly. Bake, poach, sauté, stew or steam, whole or in fillets. There are many Central European recipes – carp is eaten to celebrate Christmas Eve in many countries – and the Chinese add many interesting flavours to their carp dishes. I'm afraid in Italy carp isn't very popular, probably because of that muddy taste, and only in Vienna have I encountered it, fried in breadcrumbs, or boiled or stewed, often with celery, onion and tomato.

CARPA AL VAPORE CON CAPPERI, BURRO E LIMONE

POACHED CARP WITH CAPERS, BUTTER AND LEMON SAUCE

Carp can be steamed or poached. I poach carp at home in a *court-bouillon*, which is easy, but if you are steaming, the cooking time will be a little longer. This is a lovely dish provided you appreciate the slightly muddy flavour of the fish.

SERVES 6–8

1 carp, weighing about 2kg (4½ lb), scaled and filleted

salt and pepper to taste

Court-bouillon

1 onion

1 celery stick with leaves

1 carrot

a few bay leaves

salt and pepper

Sauce

100g (3½ oz) unsalted butter, or 100ml (3 fl oz) virgin olive oil

25g (1 oz) salted capers, prepared (see page 139), finely chopped

juice and grated zest of 1 lemon

2 tsp finely chopped fresh parsley

salt and pepper

Put the fish into a suitable pan, and cover with water. Remove the fish for the moment, and add the *court-bouillon* ingredients to the water. Bring to the boil, then lower the heat, add the fish, and simmer gently for 20 minutes. Set aside in the water.

For the sauce, melt the butter and add all the other ingredients. Heat up but do not fry. Season to taste. If you want to serve the fish cold, use olive oil instead of butter.

Bone the fish, and cut into 4 portions. Divide these between warm plates, and coat with the sauce. A good side dish would be boiled potatoes.

pesce e frutti di mare

FILETTI DI CARPA AL PANGRATTATO

FILLET OF CARP IN BREADCRUMBS

During my stay abroad, I learned a few bits and pieces of local gastronomy. This dish reminds me of when I was a student in Vienna. I often ate it in local *Gaststätten*, or *trattorie*, in the Lobau, an area of the city where the Danube forms meanders. The *gebackene Karpfen*, or fried carp, lives in my memory as a wonderful dish, which I hope I have managed to recreate properly here – decorated with fresh wild garlic.

SERVES 4

1 carp, weighing about 1.25kg (2¾ lb), scaled and filleted, cut into 4 portions

3 tbsp white wine vinegar

1 garlic clove, very finely chopped

1 tbsp very finely chopped fresh parsley

2 medium eggs, beaten

plain flour for coating

dried breadcrumbs for coating

100g (3½ oz) unsalted butter

1 lemon, quartered

salt and pepper to taste

Put the pieces of carp in a container, and add the vinegar, 1 tbsp salt and enough water to cover. Leave for an hour to take away the muddy flavour. After this time, drain and leave the fillets to dry.

Add the garlic and parsley to the beaten egg mixture. Dust the carp fillets with flour, then dip them into the egg mixture and lastly the breadcrumbs. Fry in the butter until golden brown. Serve with lemon quarters. A good accompaniment would be a salad of lamb's lettuce.

pesce e frutti di mare

LUCCIO

PIKE *Esox lucius*

The pike is a speedy and voracious hunter, eating fish (including

smaller pike), waterfowl, water-rats and frogs, and has been christened the 'barracuda of fresh water'. The European pike is found from the UK to Asia in lakes and streams, and there are several related species in North America (notably *L. niger*, or the pickerel). Pike can live for a very long time – a thirty-year-old fish has been recorded – and reach an enormous size, occasionally up to 20kg (40 lb) and over. The bigger fish are much appreciated by anglers, because they put up such a good fight, but smaller fish of about 2–2.5kg (4–5½ lb) are more convenient for the cook, and the firm white flesh is sweeter, moister and more tender. (I have a picture at home of me proudly holding a pike – a *luccio* – of around 9kg/20 lb in weight, which was caught by friends.)

The fish are long, torpedo-shaped, mottled brown and green, with a single dorsal fin towards the tail. The long pointed jaw has a wide mouth, full of very sharp teeth. When caught, the fish are covered in a slime which, from a culinary point of view, should not be washed off. The flesh can taste muddy, depending on habitat. The roes are said to be slightly toxic, but the liver is considered a delicacy. Pike need to be scaled, but the skin and scales can be removed after cooking.

It may be because of the multitude of tiny soft bones, vertical and fork-like, that pike is not eaten much in Britain; it is certainly appreciated in France, Central Europe and in Italy, particularly in Piedmont, Lombardy and Veneto. In Italy pike is usually cooked *in umido*, braised with tomatoes, or the boned fish is minced for pâtés and fish cakes. You can stuff small fish, then bake or poach them whole. In France, pike flesh is used to make terrines and mousselines, particularly the world-famous *quenelles de brochet*. I experimented with this idea, and came up with my own version – absolute heaven when served with a morel sauce.

LUCCIO IN SALSA VERDE

PIKE WITH GREEN SAUCE

The idea for this recipe comes from the Basque region of Spain, where I enjoyed *merluza in salsa verde* or cod in green sauce. To cook, you will need to use a good amount of olive oil; this imparts flavour as well as cooking the fish.

SERVES 4

4 pike steaks of about 200g (7 oz) each

olive oil

2 garlic cloves, very finely chopped

3 tbsp very finely chopped fresh parsley

lemon quarters

salt and pepper to taste

Trim the pike steaks. Pour enough olive oil to cover the steaks into a shallow pan just big enough to hold the steaks. Bring the oil up to simmering point, then add the garlic and parsley. Make sure that the oil is not too hot, then add the pike steaks. Cook over a low heat for 15 minutes or until you see little white balls forming in the oil. This is the fish protein coagulating. The oil should not bubble at all.

Drain the fish, season to taste, and serve with a spoonful of the 'green' oil, the lemon quarters and some boiled potatoes.

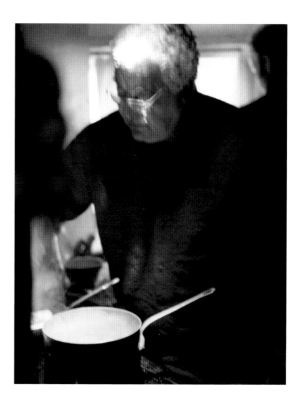

pesce e frutti di mare

CHENELLE DI LUCCIO CON SPUGNOLE

QUENELLES OF PIKE WITH MOREL SAUCE

I like the combination of fish and fungi, and this recipe works extremely well. The *quenelles* are perhaps a bit difficult to make, but it is always good to have a challenge when cooking! I have also tried the *quenelles* with a butter, lemon and dill sauce, which is excellent.

The ingredients below serve four people as a main course. Halve the recipe to serve four as a starter.

SERVES 4

400g (14 oz) fillet of pike, cleaned and completely boned

3 large egg whites

1g packet of saffron strands, or the equivalent of saffron powder

400ml (14 fl oz) double cream

salt and pepper to taste

To serve

Morel Sauce (see page 216)

1 tbsp fresh chervil leaves, plus a few extra sprigs for decoration

The *quenelles* must be prepared in a chilled environment in order to achieve success. The easiest way to ensure this is to work in a bowl sitting in a heap of ice cubes.

Place the fish fillets, egg whites, saffron and seasoning in a blender and process until completely smooth. Don't *over*beat, though; the mixture must be cold. Put into the iced bowl. In a separate bowl, whip the cream to soft peaks. Gently fold the cream into the fish mixture. Leave to chill in the fridge for a few hours.

Prepare the sauce in advance (see page 216), but add the chervil leaves after reheating.

In a wide shallow pan bring some salted water to the boil, then turn down to a simmer. With 2 dessertspoons shape the pike mixture into *quenelles*, and then lower them into the simmering water. Be very careful not to increase the temperature of the water at all. After 8–10 minutes of gentle simmering, remove the *quenelles* with a slotted spoon and drain well.

Place the *quenelles* in hot bowls on top of the warm morel sauce. Garnish with the chervil sprigs and serve immediately. This dish can be accompanied by boiled rice and a Florence fennel salad.

pesce e frutti di mare

GAMBERETTI/GAMBERI

SHRIMP AND PRAWN *Crangon crangon/Palaemon serratus*

The common or brown shrimp and the common prawn are crustaceans belonging to the same family as the lobster and crab. Both are vaguely lobster-like in shape, but very much smaller; the prawn can be about 10cm (4 in) long, the shrimp a little less. They are found inshore, the prawn in rock pools, the shrimp buried in sand (although it comes out at night), and can be difficult to spot as they are semi-translucent. Both are omnivores, but the shrimp has a particularly nasty reputation as the 'principal scavenger of the sea', eating anything and everything, usually dead, that it comes across.

Numerous varieties of prawns and shrimps come from all over the world – many of them from warm rather than cold water, and these can be very much larger. But it would be difficult to beat the flavour of the smaller cold-water varieties we find around the UK and in the Mediterranean. I think the latter have a unique fragrance of the sea, but I have been told that shrimps from Morecambe Bay in Lancashire are no less sweet.

If you are successful in the shallows with a shrimping net, take your catch straight home and plunge it into boiling salted water, preferably sea water. When the fish change colour, they are ready. You could then shell them and use the flesh in many different ways, but brown shrimps

are so good, I think they can be eaten whole unshelled. You could also flour them raw and deep-fry until crisp. I like to use them in salads, they are delicious in a Scandinavian open sandwich or a proper prawn cocktail, and shrimps potted with mace and butter, as they do in Morecambe, are delicious.

The most memorable shrimps I ever saw were in the fish market in Bombay – great heaps of a trembling translucent mass. A tiny girl was selling them, from the floor rather than from a stall! After washing the shrimps, I added a little parsley, egg and flour, and fried little heaps in olive oil until crisp. I gave the recipe to the President Hotel, part of the Taj group, and they still have it on their menu…

RAVIOLONI DI GAMBERO

PRAWN RAVIOLI

One of the most satisfactory of Italian dishes to produce is ravioli. You can use all sorts of leftovers, such as meat from roasts, stews etc. to make the filling. Here I have used a few nice prawns. To improve the taste of the sauce, cook the shells and heads in a little water. Strain and press out the juices then boil the liquid to reduce. Add to the saffron butter.

SERVES 4

Fresh Pasta (see page 104)

4 sprigs fresh dill to garnish

salt and pepper to taste

Filling

200g (7 oz) giant prawns, cooked and shelled

1 tbsp roughly chopped fresh dill

1 tbsp roughly chopped fresh parsley

2 medium egg yolks

100g (3½ oz) fresh breadcrumbs, softened in a little water

55g (2 oz) Parmesan cheese, freshly grated

Sauce

60g (2¼ oz) unsalted butter

1g packet of saffron strands, or the equivalent of saffron powder

Roll the pasta dough out to 2mm (1/16 in) thick, using a pasta machine or – much more laboriously – a rolling pin. Cut into 8cm (3¼ in) squares.

To make the filling, mince the cooked prawns with the dill, parsley, egg yolks, breadcrumbs, Parmesan and some salt and pepper to taste. Distribute the mixture over half of the pasta squares, then cover with the other pasta squares and press the outside edges together. Finish off and secure the edges using a serrated pastry wheel (or press with a fork).

Bring a large pan of water to the boil with salt (10g/¼ oz per litre/1¾ pints water). In another pan melt the sauce butter gently with the saffron. Drop the *ravioloni* one by one into the boiling water and cook for 4–5 minutes. Drain and transfer to the pan with the butter. Mix well, and serve with a sprig of dill and the butter poured over the top.

TAGLIOLINI CON GAMBERETTI

TAGLIOLINI WITH SHRIMP SAUCE

The theme of pasta and fish is used endlessly in recipes from the coastal regions of Italy. This dish, with just its few ingredients of shrimps, garlic, tomatoes, parsley and basil, is a real treat. You can use fresh home-made or bought fresh or dried pasta for this recipe. Tagliolini resemble very thin tagliatelle.

SERVES 4

250g (9 oz) shrimps, cooked

1 garlic clove, finely chopped

8 tbsp extra virgin olive oil

500g (18 oz) cherry tomatoes, coarsely chopped

1 tbsp coarsely chopped fresh flat-leaf parsley

1 tbsp coarsely chopped fresh basil

350g (12 oz) fresh tagliolini or 400g (14 oz) dried linguine

salt and pepper and/or chilli pepper to taste

Peel the shrimps, and halve or quarter if large.

Fry the garlic briefly in the olive oil, then add the shrimps and tomatoes and stir-fry for a few minutes. Then add the parsley, basil, salt and pepper and/or chilli to taste.

Meanwhile, cook the pasta in boiling salted water until *al dente* (4–5 minutes for fresh, 8–9 minutes for dried). Drain, mix with the sauce and serve immediately.

selvaggina

GAME

MAN HAS HUNTED WILD ANIMALS FOR FOOD SINCE PREHISTORIC TIMES, AND Stone Age cave and wall paintings throughout Europe record the excitement of the chase. This was the natural way of getting meat into the diet, and has remained so in theory across the Continent until the present day. In Britain, however, from very early on, the hunting, trapping and shooting of wild birds or animals became the preserve of the monarch and noblemen and, today, those who can afford to pay for a day's sport on a private estate.

The word 'game' refers to the wild animals and birds that are hunted for sport and food. I personally don't like the idea of hunting as a sport, because I don't believe killing should be considered a pleasurable experience. (I still remember live pigeons being used to prove the abilities of marksmen, a barbaric practice now replaced with 'clay' pigeons.) However, I do like the end result of the hunt – the meats of furred game such as venison, rabbit and hare, and feathered game such as grouse, partridge, pheasant, wild duck, pigeon and quail. All these are a delight to cook with and a delight to eat, as well as being healthy, for game meat is natural and lean, lower in saturated fats and lacking the possible chemicals that the flesh of farmed animals may contain. However, that said, many animals still thought of as game in Britain are now reared especially for the hunt or for the table, and there is a blurring of the previous distinction between 'wild' and 'domesticated'. Animals and birds now reared for the hunt include pheasants and partridges, while quail, pigeon, deer, rabbit and boar are actually being farmed as well as existing naturally in the wild.

In Italy, a whole range of game is eaten, from deer to the smallest wild birds. Hunting is controlled much more carefully now than it once was, but that hasn't diminished the Italian appetite – or mine – for game meat. In Britain there are strict game regulations and seasons, and I would never advise that anyone goes hunting with a gun unless with a permit and in company with a professional. There are enough licensed hunters already who provide us with supplies, and in so doing cull many of the game animals that are considered a pest by farmers (among them pigeons, rabbit, deer and wild boar). It's far better to rely on a good game dealer or specialist butcher, who can provide the meat in the proper season, with advice as to provenance, age and all the other culinary considerations. Perhaps most importantly he can prepare the animals for cooking – gutting, skinning, plucking and hanging as necessary.

Cooking and eating game are celebratory activities, and create an intimate link with that hunting instinct of the past. It may no longer be a necessity, but there still is something magical about the arrival of the proper season for a particular game animal.

selvaggina

CONIGLIO SELVATICO

WILD RABBIT *Oryctolagus cuniculus*

The rabbit is a small furred mammal native to the western Mediterranean. Rabbits were introduced to Italy by the Romans and bred as meat in special warrens known as *leporaria*. The Normans are thought to have brought rabbits to Britain and Ireland in the eleventh century – both for food and skin – and, amazingly, some authorities claim that rabbits did not become familiar in the more westerly and northerly parts of Scotland until as late as the nineteenth century. The twentieth century saw an explosion in the rabbit population, when rabbits became an agricultural pest, both in many parts of Europe and other places to which they had been introduced, such as Australia. The disease myxomatosis virtually wiped out whole populations, and numbers in the wild are still much less now than formerly.

Rabbit has long been appreciated all over Europe. In Italy it is one of the most popular meats after pork and chicken. Wild rabbit is eaten as a substitute for the gamier hare. In the mountainous regions of northern Italy, it is usually cooked with wild mushrooms and served with polenta, or it can be stewed with tomatoes, onions and garlic. Hutch or

domesticated rabbits have paler flesh and a less gamey flavour than wild, and are generally used in *ragù* sauces.

In Britain there is no season for wild rabbit, so they can be shot all year round. They are best, though, between September and November. Generally a good game dealer will supply you with rabbits of the right age, but if in doubt a young animal – which will always be the most tender – has soft ears that tear easily, white teeth, sharp claws and smooth fur. An older animal may need to be marinated and cooked very slowly to achieve tenderness. The meat of a doe (female) is generally considered superior to that of the buck (male). Rabbits do not need to be hung.

selvaggina

CONIGLIO AL FORNO

BAKED RABBIT

There exist as many versions of this dish in Italy as there are regions! Whether wild or farmed, rabbit has delicious meat, which can be compared to that of chicken and veal. I think the flavour of wild rabbit is very distinct, especially when baked or stewed.

SERVES 6–8

1kg (2¼ lb) wild rabbit on the bone (from 1 or 2 rabbits), prepared for cooking and cut into chunks

2 large onions, sliced

3 large red and 3 large yellow peppers, seeded and cut into strips

1kg (2¼ lb) waxy potatoes, thickly sliced

2 sprigs fresh rosemary

8 tbsp extra virgin olive oil

stock if necessary

salt and pepper to taste

Preheat the oven to 200°C/400°F/Gas 6.

Wash and dry the rabbit pieces and mix together with the sliced onion, pepper, potatoes, rosemary and olive oil. Season to taste. Place all the ingredients in a large casserole, and bake in the preheated oven for 30 minutes. Remove from the oven and stir all the ingredients, making sure to turn the rabbit around so that it browns evenly. Bake for a further 30 minutes, then serve immediately. If towards the end of the cooking, you feel it is too dry, add a couple of tbsp of stock. It is a complete meal in itself, very easy to prepare and cook.

selvaggina

TAGLIATELLE CON CONIGLIO, PICCIONE E PORCINI
TAGLIATELLE WITH RABBIT, PIGEON AND CEPS

Dried mushrooms combine extremely well with fresh wild mushrooms, enhancing the flavour. The combination of rabbit and pigeon with the fresh and dried ceps is irresistible. I created this recipe in the year 2000, and dedicated it to the Belgian people during a cookery demonstration for the readers of a Belgian national newspaper.

SERVES 4

150g (5½ oz) rabbit meat

150g (5½ oz) pigeon meat

100g (3½ oz) unsalted butter

2 tbsp olive oil

1 large carrot, finely chopped

1 celery stick, finely chopped

1 medium onion, finely chopped

1 garlic clove, finely chopped

6 bay leaves

50ml (2 fl oz) dry white wine

200g (7oz) fresh ceps, finely cut

25g (1 oz) dried *funghi porcini*, reconstituted (see page 102)

400g (14 oz) fresh egg tagliatelle

85g (3 oz) Parmesan cheese, freshly grated

salt and pepper to taste

Cut the rabbit meat into small strips and the wood pigeon meat into small cubes.

Place the butter, oil, carrot, celery, onion, garlic and bay leaves into a pan and fry gently until soft. Add the meat and fry for 10 minutes over a moderate heat. Add the wine and let it evaporate for 2–3 minutes. Add the fresh ceps and the chopped soaked *funghi porcini*, with 3–4 tbsp of their soaking water, and cook for another 10 minutes. Season to taste.

Cook the tagliatelle in plenty of boiling salted water for 4–5 minutes, or until *al dente*. Drain, and mix with the sauce (discarding the bay leaves). Sprinkle with Parmesan, and serve immediately.

selvaggina

LEPRE

HARE *Lepus spp*

The hare belongs to the same family as

the rabbit, the Leporidae, but the two animals are different in many ways. The hare is darker in colour, is larger, and has longer, more powerful back legs. In Italy hare is the most coveted of game, and those who manage to bag a hare are regarded as heroes. Which reminds me of a time a few years ago while I was filming in Calabria for the BBC. We had employed seven brothers, all with black bushy moustaches, to shoot a hare for the cameras. When the unfortunate animal was released from its cage, the brothers unleashed a barrage worthy of the western front, but to no avail. It was only when they let one of the dogs go in pursuit that we got our hare. This was then cooked in the rangers' hut by a very nice local woman (who also sported an incipient black moustache).

There are three species of hare in Europe. The mountain (or varying or blue) hare (*L. timidus*) is found in Scotland, Ireland, Scandinavia and the Alps, and its coat turns white in winter. The brown or European hare (*L. europaeus*) ranges all over mainland Britain and Europe (though rarer now than formerly). A third type, *L. capensis,* the Mediterranean hare, is found in Spain and many islands of the Mediterranean. In Britain, hare has an open season all year except for Sundays and Christmas Day, and may not be sold between March and July. The best time for eating it is from October to January. Leverets are animals of under a year, and they will be recognised by their tender soft ears, sharp claws, and smooth fur. They should be hung for from three to seven days.

As the blood of the hare is a major ingredient in most hare dishes, this must be retained when you shoot or buy an animal. It is much easier to let your butcher or game dealer do this for you. In a culinary sense, the main difference between hare and rabbit is that the hare has a dark rather than white meat, and it is very gamey in taste. Because of the latter, the hare should be marinated for at least 24 hours. The best meat is in the back and hind legs. The meat is also quite tough, especially in older animals, so needs slow cooking.

selvaggina

PAPPARDELLE AL SUGO DI LEPRE

PAPPARDELLE WITH HARE

This is probably one of the most classic and best loved of all Italian dishes during the hunting season. As hare is extremely difficult to shoot, I would suggest that you try to obtain one from your butcher or game dealer. A real gourmet dish, it is made even richer in some parts of Italy by the addition of a few slices of white Alba truffle. A good bottle of Barolo or Barbaresco, or even an old Chianti, would accompany this very well indeed.

SERVES 6

boned meat of ½ hare
100g (3½ oz) unsalted butter
1 medium onion, finely chopped
1 celery stick, finely diced
1 carrot, finely diced
2 sage leaves, finely chopped
2 cloves
50ml (2 fl oz) medium dry wine
1 tbsp tomato concentrate
1 tbsp bitter cocoa powder
a little freshly grated nutmeg
salt and pepper to taste

To serve

Fresh Pasta (see page 104), cut into pappardelle
55g (2 oz) Parmesan cheese, freshly grated

Make the pasta first, following the instructions on page 104. When rolled and cut, lay the fresh pasta out on a clean cloth to dry. (It is possible to buy commercial pasta of the best quality if you really have no time to make your own.)

To make the sauce, first process the hare meat in a food mixer until it resembles a medium-textured mince.

In a pan, melt 55g (2 oz) of the butter, then add the onion, celery, carrot, sage and cloves. Fry for a few minutes, then add the hare mince. When this starts to brown, after about 10–12 minutes, add the wine to the pan, followed by the tomato concentrate, cocoa powder and 2 tbsp water. Simmer for 20–30 minutes, then season with salt, pepper and nutmeg to taste.

Cook the pasta for 3–4 minutes in a large pan of boiling salted water, then drain. Transfer the pasta to a large bowl, add half the sauce, the rest of the butter and the grated Parmesan. Serve in big bowls, with the rest of the sauce poured over the top.

selvaggina

LEPRE IN SALMÍ CON POLENTA

HARE IN *SALMIS* WITH POLENTA

The lies told by hunters during the season about the size and weight of the catch are infinite. I've even heard of someone buying an already shot animal, and then making up a whole story about its fight for life!

This is the Italian version of the English jugged hare, and to complicate things even further, the word *salmis* is actually French! The polenta accompaniment is an absolute must in Piedmont.

SERVES 4

1.25kg (2¾ lb) hare meat on the bone, cut into chunks (including the blood)

55g (2 oz) plain flour

100g (3½ oz) unsalted butter

100g (3½ oz) speck or smoked *pancetta*, finely sliced

1 onion, finely chopped

4 tbsp brandy

55g (2 oz) bitter cocoa powder

salt and pepper to taste

Marinade

750ml (27 fl oz) strong red wine

1 carrot, finely diced

1 large onion, finely diced

3 celery sticks, finely diced

2 garlic cloves, finely chopped

a few fresh bay leaves

a few fresh sage leaves

a small sprig each of fresh thyme and rosemary

15 juniper berries

1 tsp black peppercorns, crushed

coarsely grated zest of ½ lemon

To serve

½ the *Polenta* recipe on page 215

Prepare the marinade first by mixing all the ingredients together. Place the hare meat in the marinade and leave for 24 or more hours, covered, in a cool place.

Remove the meat from the marinade, and leave to dry a little. Dust the meat chunks with flour and fry in the butter on all sides. Remove from the pan and set aside. Now add the speck and onion to the pan and fry until soft. Return the meat to the pan with the blood and the marinade liquid and solids. Cover and cook gently on top of the stove for 2 hours. Remove the meat and strain the liquid, discarding all the solids. Mix the brandy with a tbsp of flour. Bring the marinade liquid to the boil, then add the brandy to thicken the sauce, stirring to avoid lumps. Add the cocoa powder and salt and pepper to taste, and stir well over a gentle heat, until it thickens a little more.

Meanwhile, make the polenta, following the instructions on page 215, but *halving* the quantities.

To serve, spoon the meat and its rich gravy into warmed deep plates, and add a few spoonfuls of polenta.

selvaggina

FAGIANO

PHEASANT *Phasianus colchicus*

The pheasant is actually of eastern origin, although it has been naturalised in Europe for centuries. It is probably the most important and common game bird in Europe, but primarily because it is reared for the hunt and for the table. The exotic and gaudy colouring of the males is a familiar sight in winter, and their raucous coughing cry to their duller, smaller mates shatters the peace of many a chilly afternoon around my house in the country. Every now and again a local hunter will offer me a brace – a cock and a hen – and this gives me great pleasure, both in the cooking and eating.

The open season for pheasant in Britain is from 1 October to 1 February, and the birds are generally best from October to January. Young tender birds will have pliable beaks and feet, and can be roasted, usually well barded with *pancetta* or bacon, as the gamey dark flesh can be dry. Older birds will probably need to be stewed. The hen is considered to be the better eating. In Britain the custom is to hang the birds for some time, but in Italy we tend to use them straightaway. Good accompaniments are tart, possibly fruit, sauces – redcurrant jelly in Britain – root vegetables, wild mushrooms and polenta.

selvaggina

FAGIANO DEL BRACCONIERE

POACHER'S PHEASANT

I always imagine poachers to be good cooks, and this is the way I would cook a pheasant if I were a poacher!

SERVES 4

a brace of large pheasants, prepared for cooking

6 tbsp extra virgin olive oil

1 large onion, finely sliced

100g (3½ oz) speck, cut into small strips

3 cloves

10 juniper berries, crushed

400g (14 oz) mixed wild mushrooms (you could also add some reconstituted dried *funghi porcini* – see page 102)

2 tbsp tomato concentrate

100ml (3½ fl oz) red wine

100ml (3½ fl oz) chicken stock

salt and pepper to taste

Preheat the oven to 200°C/400°F/Gas 6.

Brown the pheasants on all sides in the oil in a large cast-iron casserole. Quarter the birds, and cut the leg and thigh pieces in half.

Fry the onion and speck for a few minutes in the same oil, then add the cloves, juniper berries, mushrooms and tomato paste. Stir-fry for a few minutes, then add the wine.

Return the pheasant pieces to the dish, pour over the stock, and season to taste with salt and pepper. Cover and braise for 1 hour in the preheated oven, then check for tenderness and seasoning. Serve with boiled rice or polenta.

selvaggina

FAGIANO CON SALSA DI MIRTILLI E MELOGRANO
PHEASANT WITH BERRY AND POMEGRANATE SAUCE

Pheasants live in the wild, but are now also raised in 'semi-domestic' fashion. In Italy we eat pheasants when freshly shot, but in Britain they are hung for up to a week to tenderise the meat. It is entirely up to personal taste.

SERVES 4

2 male pheasants, prepared for cooking

2 tbsp olive oil

4 *pancetta* or bacon rashers

salt and pepper to taste

Berry and pomegranate sauce

1 small onion, very finely sliced

85g (3 oz) unsalted butter

200g (7 oz) bilberries or blueberries

1 pomegranate, seeds only (the pulp is very bitter)

2 bay leaves

1 tbsp balsamic vinegar

1 tbsp blackberry liqueur (*mûre*)

Preheat the oven to 200°C/400°F/Gas 6.

Season the pheasants inside and out and rub the skin with olive oil. Tie the rashers of bacon or *pancetta* on to the breasts. Place the birds in a roasting dish, and roast in the preheated oven for 30 minutes.

Meanwhile, prepare the sauce by frying the onion in the butter until soft. Add the berries, pomegranate seeds and bay leaves and fry for 10 minutes, or until the berries are soft. Add the balsamic vinegar and blackberry liqueur, and season to taste with salt and pepper. Leave to simmer for a few minutes, to let the alcohol evaporate.

Remove the pheasants from the oven, and lift the *pancetta* off the breast, keeping it aside to garnish. Carve the birds, serving half a bird per person, and arrange on hot plates accompanied by the sauce. Garnish with the bay leaves and *pancetta*. Good vegetables to serve with this dish would be deep-fried parsnip ribbons or croquette potatoes.

selvaggina

GALLO CEDRONE

GROUSE *Lagopus lagopus scoticus*

I am passionate about seasonality in foods, and grouse, perhaps the most revered of all game birds, is uniquely seasonal. For one particular date, the 'Glorious Twelfth' of August, is when the grouse shooting season begins. Although it may not be so glorious for the birds themselves, it is for gourmets the whole country over.

The grouse in question is the red grouse, which is only found in Scotland, Ireland and some more northerly parts of England and Wales. It has many other European relations, though, including the willow grouse, the capercaillie (wood grouse), ptarmigan (white grouse) and the black grouse. Although all varieties are eaten, the red is considered to be the aristocrat, probably because it is truly wild, existing on a diet of ling heather and berries, which gives its flesh a pungent, rich gaminess. In a good season, when food has been abundant, the breasts will be thick and tender.

The season extends from 12 August to 10 December in Britain, and the birds are best between August and October. They should be hung for between two and four days. Young birds with pliable beaks and claws, and pointed wing tips, need only simple roasting, well barded with *pancetta*, bacon or pork fat. In my restaurant I like to serve them still slightly pink with sautéed chanterelles. Other accompaniments might be a berry sauce, possibly of berries on which the bird itself might have fed – bilberries, raspberries or rowan berries. Older birds need to be slowly cooked, pot-roasted or braised. I also use grouse meat in pies, terrines and pâtés.

Shooting grouse is a very expensive sport, and many large Scottish estates are populated with people from all over Europe during the month of August. I know of one party of Italians who organised a shooting party in Scotland. Halfway through the beating, they abandoned the hunt to dedicate themselves to the much more pleasurable pursuit of collecting wild mushrooms. Men after my own heart!

selvaggina

PÂTÉ DI GALLO CEDRONE

GROUSE PÂTÉ

Pâtés in the past used up surplus or leftover ingredients, and in the process many excellent new dishes were created. For this dish, I had leftover duck and venison which, in tandem with the grouse, ensure a very gamey flavour indeed.

SERVES 4

500g (18 oz) raw breast of grouse, coarsely minced

300g (10½ oz) each of raw wild duck and venison meat, minced

400g (14 oz) pork back (*lardo*), minced

4 tbsp brandy

½ tsp freshly grated nutmeg

unsalted butter and dried breadcrumbs for the terrine

2 medium eggs

2 tbsp double cream

8 juniper berries, crushed

3 shallots, finely diced

20 fresh bay leaves

salt and pepper

Marinate the minced meats with the brandy, nutmeg and some salt and pepper for 2 hours.

Preheat the oven to 180°C/350°F/Gas 4. Grease a 1.5 litre (2¾ pint) terrine dish with butter and sprinkle with breadcrumbs.

Beat the eggs, then add the cream, juniper berries, shallot and salt and pepper to taste. Mix the minced meats with this egg mixture until well blended.

Cover the walls of the terrine with bay leaves, then pour in the meat mixture and smooth down. Cover with the lid or foil, and bake in a *bain-marie* in the preheated oven for about 2 hours. Leave to cool in the oven, and chill for a day before using.

selvaggina

GALLO CEDRONE CON FINFERLI

GROUSE WITH CHANTERELLES

I couldn't think of a better combination of two of my favourite wild foods. The grouse is incomparable, much more sought after than other game birds, and to accompany it is the fungus most appreciated by gourmets all over the world. In this case, both originate from Scotland, where wild food seems to be in abundance.

SERVES 4

4 grouse, prepared for cooking
olive oil
25g (1 oz) unsalted butter
12 bay leaves
24 slices *pancetta*, about 200g (7 oz)
salt and pepper to taste

Chanterelles
1 small onion, finely chopped
55g (2 oz) unsalted butter
500g (18 oz) fresh chanterelles, cleaned and trimmed
1 tbsp chopped fresh parsley

Preheat the oven to 200°C/400°F/Gas 6.

Brush the birds with a little olive oil, and season with salt and pepper on both the skin and inside the cavity. Transfer two at a time to a frying pan and fry in half the butter each time over a high heat, for 5 minutes on each side. Remove the birds from the pan and keep to one side.

Place 3 bay leaves inside the cavity of each grouse, and cover the breast of each with 6 slices of *pancetta*. Place the birds in the preheated oven and roast for 15 minutes.

Meanwhile, fry the onion in the butter until transparent, then add the chanterelles, frying them for a few minutes. Season with salt and pepper.

Serve the birds immediately they are ready, accompanied by the chanterelles sprinkled with the chopped parsley. A bottle of old Barolo or Barbaresco will go very well with this dish.

selvaggina

ANATRA SELVATICA

WILD DUCK *Anas spp*

The duck has been domesticated for some 2,000 years: this began in China, and duck is still a favoured meat there. The ancestor of all present-day domesticated ducks is the mallard (*Anas platyrhynchos*), still the most common wild duck in Europe at least, and it is also the most popular in a culinary sense. Also classified as good for eating are the wild ducks known as teal (*A. crecca*), the smallest duck in Britain, and wigeon or widgeon (*A. penelope*). Other ducks have been trapped or shot for food over the centuries, and these include the pintail, shelduck, gadwall and shoveller.

The primary consideration so far as eating wild duck is concerned is its palatability, for the flesh can take on very unpleasant, often fishy, flavours. This is entirely dependent on habitat and diet (although time of year and age come into it too). The ducks which feed in fresh water, and which are primarily vegetarian, are less fishy and oily in flavour than those which live and eat in and on salt water. Interestingly, in the days when eating meat was forbidden during Lent, pintail and teal were allowed in the diet (because more maritime and fishy in nature?), but not mallard.

In Italy we love ducks in general, and we are very keen wildfowlers in the autumn, pursuing the *anatra selvatica* in particular. Wild duck are not hung for very long in Italy, and even in Britain – where some game birds are hung almost to putrefaction – many experts do not recommend hanging. After plucking and cleaning, the birds are best roasted quickly until still quite pink – Tom Stobart in his masterly *Cook's Encyclopedia* says: ' …a mallard should walk through the kitchen, a widgeon should run slowly through, and a teal should rush through'! They can also be braised. Accompaniments are usually sharp to complement the oily, gamey flesh – a bitter or Seville orange sauce, a port gravy or apple sauce – and my crab apple and horseradish relish is just the thing (see page 88).

selvaggina

PETTI DI ANATRA SELVATICA CON TARTUFO NERO
BREAST OF WILD DUCK WITH BLACK TRUFFLE

This is an extravagant recipe because it requires only the breast of duck (as well as a truffle, of course!). However, I suggest that you roast the entire duck, and use the rest of the meat (well minced) to make a ravioli stuffing.

SERVES 4

2 wild ducks, prepared for cooking

4 tbsp olive oil

1 garlic clove, finely sliced

55g (2 oz) unsalted butter

1 black truffle, cut into small strips

2 tbsp balsamic vinegar

a few drops of white truffle oil

salt and pepper to taste

Preheat the oven to 180°C/350°F/Gas 4.

Brush the ducks with some of the olive oil, and season with salt and pepper outside and inside. Roast for 40 minutes in the preheated oven until tender. Leave to rest while you prepare the sauce.

Fry the garlic in the rest of the olive oil with the butter, then add the truffle and vinegar, cooking for a couple of minutes. Add the drops of truffle oil, and season to taste.

Cut the breasts off the birds and transfer to hot plates. Pour over the truffle sauce. This dish can be accompanied by boiled spinach and fried potatoes.

selvaggina

ANATRA ARROSTO CON MELINE AL RAFANO

ROAST DUCK WITH CRAB APPLE AND HORSERADISH RELISH

This is when the crab apple relish on page 88 will come into its own! It combines very well with any kind of game, but is ideal with duck, as duck is usually served with a similar sweet/sour sauce.

SERVES 4

1 large wild duck or 2 smaller wild duck, prepared for cooking
juice of 1 lemon
2 sprigs fresh rosemary
4 tbsp olive oil
55g (2 oz) unsalted butter
1 tbsp balsamic vinegar

1 tsp cornflour, diluted in a little hot water
salt and pepper to taste

To serve
4 tbsp *Crab Apple and Horseradish Relish* (see page 88)

Preheat the oven to 180°C/350°F/Gas 4. Sprinkle some lemon juice into the cavity of the bird(s), then season inside and out with salt and pepper. Place the rosemary in the cavity, then brush all over with the olive oil. Roast the smaller ducks in the preheated oven for 20–25 minutes until tender and juicy, the larger one for 40–50 minutes. Set aside to rest.

Add 2 tbsp water to the roasting juices in the roasting tin, and heat and stir to loosen the roasting residues. Transfer to a pan, and add the butter and vinegar, followed by the cornflour liquid. Cook for a couple of minutes, then strain.

Carve the duck(s), and serve on hot plates with the sauce poured over and the relish at the side. A good accompaniment is boiled potatoes.

selvaggina

PERNICE

PARTRIDGE *Perdix perdix/Alectoris rufa*

Many varieties of partridge exist throughout the world, but two are particularly common and popular as food throughout Europe. The largest and possibly the most numerous is the red-legged partridge (*Alectoris rufa*); the other is the smaller, grey-legged partridge (*Perdix perdix*). In Italy, both of these – *pernice rossa* and *pernice grigia* or *starna* respectively – are joined by a third, the yellow-legged partridge (*A. barbara*) which is only found in Sardinia (and North Africa). The grey-legged is native to Britain and is the more popular both because of its flavour and because it flies when disturbed (sadly, in family groups or coveys), thus making for exciting shooting. The red-legged, introduced from France to Britain throughout the seventeenth to the nineteenth centuries, is less attractive in flavour to the British, although it's very highly prized by the French and Italians. It also tends to run rather than fly when disturbed, so isn't nearly such a challenge to marksmen.

Partridge, of the same family as quail and pheasant, are one of the most common of game birds, and are in season in Britain from 1 September to 1 February. Like pheasant, they can be reared on the big estates. They should be hung for two to three days maximum in my opinion (some British books recommend a week), and then they are best roasted, but it all depends on age. As the birds are so small – no more than 450g (1 lb) each – serve one per person. I like to cook and purée the livers of the birds, spread them on a *crostini* or piece of toast, and serve the roast bird on top of this. Accompaniments, as with most game, are tart and/or fruity.

selvaggina

CROSTINI CON PERNICE

PARTRIDGE *CROSTINI*

This will be a real delicacy for lovers of Tuscan *crostini*. Chicken liver pâté is usually used, but I discovered that partridge, although not so economical perhaps, produced a splendid culinary result. If you want to impress dinner-party guests with your culinary skills, then this is your chance …

SERVES 4

4 partridges, prepared for cooking, with livers

olive oil

12 slices Tuscan or good white country bread

extra virgin olive oil for brushing

salt and pepper to taste

Marinade

3 salted anchovy fillets, prepared (see below)

250ml (9 fl oz) strong red wine

6 tbsp olive oil

5 fresh sage leaves

a few sprigs of fresh rosemary

15g (½ oz) salted capers, prepared (see page 139)

1 garlic clove, finely chopped

To prepare the salted anchovies, soak them in a little water and vinegar for 15 minutes to soften them, then remove the bones. Drain well, then chop and mix with all the other marinade ingredients in a stainless-steel bowl. Season with salt and pepper. Immerse the partridges in this liquid for 24 hours.

When you wish to cook, preheat the oven to 200°C/400°F/Gas 6. Remove the partridges from the marinade, pat them dry, and brush with olive oil. Roast them in the preheated oven for 15 minutes. Remove from the oven, leave to cool a little, then remove the flesh from the bones. Keep this and the livers.

Remove the herbs from the marinade. Put the marinade and the partridge meat into a pan, and cook over a gentle heat for 10 minutes, stirring from time to time. Put everything into a blender and reduce to a paste. Add salt and pepper to taste.

Toast the bread and, while still warm, brush with a little extra virgin olive oil. Spread some of the partridge pâté on the toast, and wait for the compliments!

selvaggina

LA PERNICE CON LA PERA

THE PARTRIDGE AND THE PEAR

I have to admit that during my twenty-five years in Britain, I have taken on a little 'Britishness', one facet of which is the name of this recipe, in honour of the famous Christmas song, 'A partridge in a pear tree'. The combination of partridge and pear has always been loved, and not only by my English customers…

SERVES 4

4 partridges, prepared for cooking, ready barded
    if possible, plus giblets
55g (2 oz) unsalted butter
1 tbsp brandy
100ml (3½ fl oz) chicken broth
salt and pepper to taste

Pears

2 pears, not too ripe (William)
10 cloves
4 grates of nutmeg
2.5cm (1 in) cinnamon stick
100g (3½ oz) caster sugar
40ml (1½ fl oz) white wine vinegar
4 tbsp water

First prepare the pears. Peel them, halve them and remove the cores. Put all the remaining pear ingredients into a saucepan, add some salt and pepper and bring to the boil. Immerse the pears in this liquid and cook for 15 minutes, depending on their initial texture. We want them to still be quite firm. Allow to cool.

Preheat the oven to 200°C/400°F/Gas 6. Remove the liver and giblets from the partridges and put them to one side. Salt and pepper the birds inside and out.

Heat a casserole thoroughly on top of the stove, and then add half the butter, which should melt immediately. Place the partridges and their giblets in the pan and fry over a high heat to seal in the juices for 5 minutes on each side. Throw away the barding fat, and remove the giblets and liver which should be cooked by now. Replace the partridges in the pan together with the remaining butter, the brandy and the broth. Roast in the hot oven for 15–20 minutes.

When cooked, remove the partridges and keep them warm while you make the sauce using the partridge juices. Purée the liver and giblets and stir into the roasting juices over a low flame, then season with salt and pepper.

Serve the partridges with the pears and a little sauce. Ideal vegetables to serve with this dish are potato and cheese croquettes and baked celery, which can be cooked in the hot oven at the same time.

selvaggina

PICCIONE/COLOMBACCIO

WOOD PIGEON *Columba palumbus*

selvaggina

Many people in Britain dislike the idea of eating pigeon because they think they might have to ingest something resembling the battered, grubby birds that fight over grain and bread in city streets from San Marco in Venice to London's Trafalgar Square. This common pigeon is a descendant of the rock dove, and indeed these are the birds which are farmed today all over Europe. No, what you eat as pigeon is wood pigeon, that elegant, colourful and plump bird which you find all through the European countryside, and even occasionally see in city parks. In fact, the whole British attitude to pigeon amazes me. During the Middle Ages in Britain (and probably even earlier), pigeons were bred as food (an introduction from the Romans, of course); every household of some size had a pigeon loft or dovecote. But wood pigeons are considered a pest now by most farmers in Britain, and it is true that they can strip many a crop, from cereals to potatoes to turnips. They do the same in France and Italy, of course, but we tend to accept that this is nature, and think of higher things – like how good they will taste eventually in the pot!

The *piccione* or *colombaccio* has a greater reputation in Italy than the farmed variety. The dark gamey flesh of older birds has a wonderful flavour; the gaminess is still apparent, though, in the flesh of squabs, young pigeons of often no older than four weeks. You can tell the age of a pigeon by the beak: the younger the bird, the more elastic its beak will be. Young birds can be roasted – but bard the breasts well to prevent drying – while older birds will need to be braised. There's a marvellous Venetian soup, *sopa coada* – its main ingredients braised pigeons and bread – but I like pigeons stuffed or braised with olives, the latter a famous recipe which uses both wild or farmed birds.

COLOMBACCIO RIPIENO

STUFFED WOOD PIGEON

Stuffing boned birds is an unusual way of preparing game. It is easier to bone a chicken or duck, but with a little patience and a sharp knife, you should be able to bone your own birds. However, in case you find yourself totally incapable, then persuade your trusted game dealer or butcher to do it for you.

SERVES 4

4 boned wood pigeons
8 thin slices *pancetta*
4 tbsp extra virgin olive oil
salt and pepper to taste

Stuffing
85g (3 oz) fresh white breadcrumbs
2 medium eggs, beaten
85g (3 oz) mortadella, cut into little cubes
3 tbsp coarsely chopped fresh flat-leaf parsley
30g (1¼ oz) Parmesan cheese, freshly grated

Sauce
50g (1¾ oz) butter
4 tbsp balsamic vinegar

Preheat the oven to 180°C/350°F/Gas 4.

Combine all the stuffing ingredients, mixing well, then season with salt and pepper. Stuff into the cavities of the birds. Cover the breasts with 2 slices *pancetta* per bird, and fix with wooden cocktail sticks. Brush the birds with the olive oil, and roast, breast down, in the preheated oven for 15 minutes. Turn over, breasts up, and roast for a further 15 minutes. Baste with the cooking juices.

Make the sauce by melting the butter in a pan. When melted and hot, add the balsamic vinegar and some black pepper. Let it evaporate a little.

Serve the pigeons on hot plates with a little of the sauce, and accompanied by baked potatoes or spinach.

selvaggina

PICCIONE CON LE OLIVE

WOOD PIGEON WITH OLIVES

Piccione con le olive is a classic Italian dish from the Tuscan and Ligurian regions. Because finding wood pigeon is becoming more and more difficult, the domesticated variety is often used.

SERVES 4

4 wood pigeons, prepared for cooking, with livers

4 tbsp Ligurian olive oil

100ml (3½ fl oz) chicken stock

1 large onion, finely sliced

1 carrot, finely sliced

55g (2 oz) unsalted butter

4 bay leaves

a sprig of fresh rosemary

100g (3½ oz) Taggiasca olives (small Ligurian olives), pitted

100ml (3½ fl oz) Vin Santo or sherry

salt and pepper to taste

Preheat the oven to 200°C/400°F/Gas 6.

Rub some of the olive oil over the pigeons, then season them inside and out with salt and pepper. Roast in the preheated oven for 20 minutes, then leave to cool. When cool enough to handle, cut the meat off the breasts, legs and thighs. Put the carcasses in the stock, bring to the boil and boil for 10-15 minutes. Remove the bones and reduce a little more. Strain and season to taste.

Fry the onion and carrot in the butter and remaining oil until soft. Add the pigeon meat, the bay leaves, strained, reduced stock, rosemary and olives to the pan and heat through. Add the Vin Santo or sherry and continue to cook for 10 minutes on a low heat. Adjust the seasoning (not too much salt, though, because of the cured olives), and serve hot, with mashed potatoes or simply some bread.

selvaggina

QUAGLIA

QUAIL *Coturnix coturnix*

The quail is the smallest game bird in Europe, and it is also the only one which is migratory. As winter approaches, it flies from the cooler north to India and Africa, returning only in the spring to breed. On the way, over the years, they have been netted in huge quantities, particularly in Italy, then fattened for the pot. Wild stocks are now rather diminished, perhaps as a result of that continental greed. In fact, it is illegal to hunt wild quail in Britain, but as the birds are easy to breed on farms, quail is now almost as familiar and popular a food in Britain as it is in France and Italy. Quails' eggs are increasingly common too. Apparently hen quails can start laying when only about six weeks old, and lay at least one egg a day. In the wild, individual nests can hold up to eighteen eggs, but this is thought to be due to the efforts of more than one female, as male quails are said to be inclined to bigamy…

A member of the partridge family, the quail looks very like a miniature partridge. Only about 18cm (7 in) long, they weigh about 150g (5½ oz) each. Two birds at least will be needed per person, and I think roasting is best, well barded with bacon. (Then, unless they are boned, you can eat them in your fingers – one of my favourite modes of eating.) They can also be stewed or grilled. The flesh of farmed quail is not so gamey as wild, but it is still delicious, and it does not need to be hung. Serve with wild mushrooms and/or polenta or, as the Tuscans do, part roasted then grilled on a skewer with pieces of bread between to catch the luscious juices.

selvaggina

INSALATA DI FUNGHI E QUAGLIE

QUAIL AND FUNGI SALAD

Quail are probably the smallest birds that the British will eat without feeling like 'baby snatchers'. Of course the Italians eat birds that are much smaller, such as sparrows or thrushes, and although I have tasted the forbidden *volatili* in my youth, I do actually prefer slightly bigger birds such as quail. We shall leave the consumption of songbirds to a few hunters and gourmets in Lombardy and the Veneto …

SERVES 4

4 large quails, prepared for cooking

6 tbsp extra virgin olive oil

2 thick slices Parma ham, cut into strips

200g (7 oz) oyster mushrooms

300g (10½ oz) mixed salad leaves

juice of ½ lemon

salt and pepper to taste

Preheat the oven to 200°C/400°F/Gas 6.

Brush the quails with some of the olive oil, then season the birds inside and out with salt and pepper. Roast in the preheated oven for 16–18 minutes. Leave to cool, then while still warm, carve the meat off the breasts, legs and thighs.

Pour the rest of the oil in to a pan and fry the Parma ham briefly, then add the mushrooms. Stir-fry for 6–7 minutes. Add the quail pieces to warm through.

Arrange the salad leaves on plates. Add the lemon juice to the quail, fungi, ham and oil, then season to taste. Arrange this mixture over the salad. Serve warm, accompanied by *grissini* (breadsticks), *tarallucci* (round savoury biscuits), or toasted *crostini*.

selvaggina

LE QUAGLIE DI GIULIETTA

JULIET'S QUAILS

Juliet Glyn Smith was a very good friend of my wife and myself. When she died many years ago, sadly prematurely, she left me with a culinary conundrum. Invariably when invited to large parties at her house in Richmond, the already jolly Juliet would show me a large black pot full of what appeared to be boiled quails. I can't now ever find out what her intentions were, but I was always invited to try and improve on the dish. This recipe is an approximation of what I achieved a couple of times, and I dedicate it to her memory.

SERVES 4

8 quails, prepared for cooking

plain flour for coating

olive oil for frying

1 carrot, very finely sliced

2 celery sticks, very finely diced

1 onion, very finely chopped

juice and coarsely grated rind of 1 lemon

a few bay leaves

250ml (9 fl oz) dry white wine

3 grates of nutmeg

salt and pepper to taste

Season the quails inside and out. Coat them with plain flour and fry in 4 tsp oil in a large ovenproof pot with a lid for a few minutes on each side until brown. Remove. Fry the carrot, celery and onion in the same pot until soft. Add the lemon rind and juice. Fry for a few more minutes, and then add the bay leaves, wine, nutmeg and salt and pepper to taste. Add the quails to the pot in one layer. Cover the pan, and cook on top of the stove for about 20 minutes.

To serve, cut away the breast and the thighs and line up on the plate. Pour the sauce over the top. You can also eat them as we used to at Juliet's dinner parties: take them one by one in your hand and chew off as much meat as you can. It's very messy!

selvaggina

CERVO

VENISON *Capreolus capreolus* (Roe), *Dama dama* (Fallow), *Cervus elaphus* (Red)

Venison, the meat of deer, is the king of game, and hunting deer is the game of kings. The name in English comes from Latin *venaria* or hunting, and indeed from Roman times special game preserves were established all over Europe. Kings and aristocrats maintained hunting lodges and set aside huge tracts of forest and plain over which they could pursue their sport. By the thirteenth century one-third of England, for instance, is said to have been turned into a royal hunting ground.

Red deer, roe deer and fallow deer are the wild species most commonly available in Europe, each with their own open seasons in Britain. The French and Italians like roe best (the red is virtually extinct in Italy), while the red seems to be favoured in Britain, where they are farmed. Eating venison is not a pleasure to be enjoyed only by the rich, because farmed meat is now available in supermarkets. Inevitably, of course, there is some loss of flavour and texture, but farmed venison is still extremely low-fat and healthy protein. The best parts come from the haunch and saddle, preferably from an animal no older than two years, and it should be hung for up to about ten days. These cuts are best roasted, whilst the neck and other parts are better stewed or made into a *ragù*. It all depends on the age, though, and you must rely on a trustworthy game dealer. Deer in the wild can be shot at any age up to fifteen years or more, which can mean a tough and indigestible flesh.

Venison is best in autumn, when the deer have fattened on the abundant food supplies of the summer – grass and, occasionally, to the farmers' and gardeners' rage, field crops and garden foliage. Because the meat is so dense, it can be very dry, and so is usually marinated first, for at least a few hours in wine, olive oil, herbs and spices, often with juniper berries, the classic game flavouring. Then, according to the cut, it can be casseroled or slow-roasted with a further protection of barding fat, *pancetta* or bacon. As I can reliably get hold of young animals, I can cook prime pieces of venison, such as the fillet, and I love to serve wild mushrooms with them, as all are available at the same time of year. Tart fruit sauces are a good accompaniment, as with all game.

selvaggina

SPEZZATINO DI CERVO CON POLENTA E FUNGHI

VENISON STEW WITH POLENTA AND FUNGI

A venison or hare stew (see page 191) is best accompanied by wet polenta, the famous 'porridge' made with yellow or white maize. Any dish with a sauce needs something to absorb the juices (usually rice or potatoes), but game needs a stronger accompaniment like polenta, to match the flavours.

SERVES 8–10

1.8kg (4 lb) venison meat, preferably from the haunch
plain flour for coating
100ml (3½ fl oz) olive oil
55g (2 oz) dried *funghi porcini*, reconstituted (see page 102), then chopped
100g (3½ oz) speck, cut into strips
½ tsp nutmeg, freshly ground
100g (3½ oz) tomato concentrate
salt and pepper to taste

Marinade

1 litre (1¾ pints) strong red wine
1 tbsp juniper berries, crushed

1 tsp black peppercorns, coarsely crushed
4 bay leaves
1 sprig fresh rosemary
2 garlic cloves, crushed
coarsely chopped rind of 1 lemon
2 carrots, finely chopped
1 onion, finely chopped

Polenta

600g (1 lb 5 oz) maize flour (or pre-cooked polenta)
3 litres (5¼ pints) water
100g (3½ oz) Parmesan cheese, freshly grated
100g (3½ oz) unsalted butter
salt to taste

Place all the ingredients for the marinade into a stainless-steel bowl. Cut the meat into chunks and place in the marinade. Season to taste with salt and pepper, then leave for 24 hours, covered in a cool place. Pick out the meat, and put to one side. Strain the marinade and reserve the liquid.

Dry the meat then dust with flour. Heat the olive oil in a large pan and fry the venison on all sides until golden. Remove the meat. Add the chopped *funghi porcini* and speck, and fry briefly. Add the nutmeg and tomato concentrate along with 100ml (3½ fl oz) of the *porcini* water and all the marinade (except for the lemon rind and rosemary), then bring to the boil. Add the meat, reduce the heat, cover, and simmer for an hour. Add more of the soaking water from the *funghi porcini* if necessary and cook for another hour or until the meat is tender. The venison should be very moist with plenty of sauce.

Meanwhile, cook the polenta. (If using the quick polenta, then follow the instructions on the packet.) Bring the water to the boil, add plenty of salt, then gradually add the maize flour, stirring continuously with a wooden spoon. Incorporate all the flour without any lumps forming. Continue to stir until smooth and the polenta is starting to come away from the side of the pan, which should take about 30–40 minutes. (Quick polenta should take about 5 minutes, but in my opinion does not have as much flavour.) Mix the Parmesan and butter into the polenta. Serve the stew in deep plates, with a few spoonfuls of polenta.

CERVO CON SPUGNOLE

VENISON WITH MOREL SAUCE

This is one of the most popular dishes on my restaurant menu in the autumn and winter. To ensure tenderness, the best cut to use is the fillet, but unfortunately this is also the most expensive. This morel sauce also goes very well with the *quenelles* of pike on page 177.

SERVES 4

500g (18 oz) fillet of venison, trimmed and cut into 1cm (½ in) thick medallions
2 tbsp extra virgin olive oil
salt and pepper to taste

Marinade

3 tbsp extra virgin olive oil
1 tbsp balsamic vinegar (non-aged)
1 carrot, finely diced
1 celery stick, finely diced
1 onion, finely diced

Morel sauce

55g (2 oz) dried morels, soaked in warm water for 2 hours (reserve the water)
2 small onions, very finely sliced
100g (3½ oz) unsalted butter
2 tbsp balsamic vinegar (aged for 10–15 years)
4 tbsp dry sherry
6 tbsp double cream

The day before cooking, place the venison in a dish and cover with the marinade ingredients. Season with salt and pepper. (The vegetables from the marinade can be used afterwards in a sauce for rice or pasta.)

To make the sauce, fry the onion in the butter until transparent. Add the pre-soaked morels and cook for 10–15 minutes, then add the balsamic vinegar, sherry, cream and some salt and pepper. Cook gently for a further 10 minutes. You may need to thin the sauce at this stage: add a little of the morel soaking water to the pan.

Season the venison and then fry for 3 minutes on each side in the oil, until brown on the outside, pink on the inside. Spoon the sauce and morels on to a hot plate, and then place the venison on top. A perfect accompaniment would be some wet polenta (see page 215).

selvaggina

CINGHIALE

WILD BOAR *Sus scropha*

The wild pig or boar has been hunted since the dawning of man,

and forms of the animal exist across Asia and Europe. It has been extinct in Britain since the seventeenth century, but can still be found in many parts of Italy and elsewhere in Europe. The ancestor of the modern pork pig, it is still hunted in its own environment. In Tuscany and Umbria, boar hunting is a major sport, and the animal is much sought after in the undergrowth where it hides, nibbling away at tender juicy foliage shoots and berries (it can damage crops). Elsewhere there are farms which rear semi-wild boar; these are crossbreeds, coming from Portugal and Spain. Their flesh is less gamey than the truly wild animal.

The meat of wild boar is much valued by French and Italian chefs alike, being very dense in texture, red in colour (it is not bled like pork pigs), low in fat and cholesterol, and high in protein. It can be used in a variety of ways, from stews or roasts, to air-cured hams and fresh or air-dried sausages. In Italy they serve a wild boar ham, coated with its own black bristly skin, *prosciutto di cinghiale*. Wild boar's very distinctive flavour makes it ideal for a *ragù* sauce to flavour special pastas such as *pinci* or *ceriole*, a Tuscan speciality. In Italian delicatessens you often find wild boar sausages kept in an oil-filled jar, which are ideal when eaten as *antipasto*, accompanied by a strong red Tuscan wine.

The hunting season for wild boar is the autumn, but farmed boar is available all year round. It is now possible to buy wild boar in specialised butchers' shops throughout the country.

selvaggina

SCOTTIGLIA DI CINGHIALE

TUSCAN WILD BOAR STEW

In Tuscany towards the autumn, you will invariably find this dish on the menu in local *trattorie*, eaten simply with bread as a main course. *Scottiglia* is a very comforting wild boar stew. In fact, the Tuscans love it so much that in season they freeze parts of the animal so that they can make this stew later in the year – and Italians do not tend to freeze very much. Depending on the age of the boar, it can take some time to tenderise the meat, but a *scottiglia* is always cooked slowly to avoid toughening the meat. This type of stew can be made with other, more tender parts of the animal, but reduce the cooking time accordingly.

SERVES 4

1 kg (2¼ lb) wild boar meat, cut into chunks

plain flour for dusting

100ml (3½ fl oz) olive oil

2 carrots, finely sliced

1 large onion, finely chopped

2 celery sticks, finely diced

2 garlic cloves, finely chopped

4 fresh bay leaves

1 chilli, chopped

100ml (3½ fl oz) dry white or red wine

800g (1 lb 12 oz) ripe tomato pulp (either from skinned tomatoes or bought in cartons)

1 sprig fresh rosemary

salt and pepper to taste

Dust the meat pieces in flour, and shake off the excess. Brown on all sides in the oil in a large casserole. Add the vegetables, garlic, bay leaves and chilli and cook slowly until soft, about 15 minutes. Add the wine and let it evaporate. Add the tomatoes and leave to cook slowly, covered, for a couple of hours. Add some water if necessary during this time.

Just before the end of cooking time, add the rosemary, salt and abundant pepper. Check for tenderness and seasoning. Serve hot with Tuscan bread or boiled potatoes.

selvaggina

COTOLETTA DI CINGHIALE PEPERONI AGRO DOLCE
WILD BOAR CUTLET WITH SWEET AND SOUR PEPPERS

Italians enjoy the meat of pig very much, whether wild or domesticated, and the marriage of this meat with sweet and sour peppers makes for a very successful taste experience.

SERVES 4

4 large wild boar cutlets

10 tbsp olive oil

4 yellow peppers, seeded and cut into strips

4 red peppers, seeded and cut into strips

3 garlic cloves, coarsely chopped

1 tbsp caster sugar

4 tbsp white wine vinegar

salt and pepper to taste

Fry the cutlets in the oil in a large pan over a medium heat for 10 minutes on each side, or until golden. Set aside and keep warm.

In the same pan and in the same oil, fry the pepper strips for 10 minutes, stirring frequently, then add the garlic and fry for a further 5 minutes. Add the sugar, vinegar and salt and pepper to taste. Stir well, then pour over the cutlets and serve immediately.

selvaggina

Index

Note: Page numbers in **bold** refer to major text sections, those in *italic* to illustrations of recipes. Vegetarian dishes include dairy products and eggs, and are given in **bold**.

indice

indice